WINNING WITH ARTIFICIAL INTELLIGENCE

Seven Points Business Leaders Don't Know about Competing With A.I.

Dr. Militza Basualdo

Table of Contents

INTRODUCTION

The year is 2016.

The world champion of the game of Go, Lee Sedol, and an artificial intelligence, AlphaGo, were having a match in South Korea. The event was being transmitted over multiple media channels, with more than 200 million persons attending. The event took place in South Korea when it was nighttime in the Americas. Even with the inconvenient time, many in the Americas watched the tournament.

The match between Lee Sedol and the machine started like any regular tournament. The tournament was a five-game event. AlphaGo won the first three games, and Lee Sedol won the fourth game. The fifth game is now part of AI history. After 280 moves in the fifth game, AlphaGo made an unexpected move, placing a stone on the board's lower-left side. At first sight, everyone thought the machine had made a mistake and even double-checked the instructions from AlphaGo. No human had made that type of move before. Lee Sedol looked at the board in disbelief and then in anguish. He became desperate. He left the event abruptly to go outside. After a few minutes, he returned to the tournament, stared at the board for 15 minutes, and sadly accepted defeat.

Go is a popular game played in Asia. The game has more possible moves than the number of atoms in the universe. To prepare for the game, the artificial intelligence AlphaGo, only received the rules of the game. AlphaGo learned to play Go by first watching 150,000 games, analyzing 30 million moves in the process, and then playing itself against previous versions of itself[1]. After 21 days of learning by itself, AlphaGo could beat 60 Go experts. After 40 days, AlphaGo became the best Go player in the world.

The tournament proved that artificial intelligence could become an expert learning by itself. The business world has not been the same since that event.

A new way of doing business today

Savvy corporations use the new artificial intelligence, AI, capabilities to compete in new ways that previously had not been possible. Using AI's ability to learn, companies now have detailed insights into each customer's preferences and offer personalized services. Chatbots can quickly answer customers' questions at any time. Some banks can process loan requests and provide an answer in less than a minute. Grocery warehouses can operate with autonomous robots to fulfill orders. AI algorithms can predict trends, set prices, and optimize inventories. Through AI predictive analytics insights, B2B salespersons can reduce customer churn and increase cross-selling. AI can reduce costs and increase revenues and employee engagement. Artificial intelligence is not only a tool for differentiation in this digital age but a tool for making corporations competitive.

Leaders are implementing AI but failing to obtain the full benefits

Many leaders want to use AI for business. Successful 21st Century companies are already enjoying high profitability with AI. When executives decide to use AI, many simply request Information Technology, IT, to implement it. After spending considerable time, effort, and money, the company finds only minimal benefits. Management becomes frustrated and wonders what they did wrong or if AI is the right technology for them. Over half the companies who implement AI experience little or no benefits.

Low returns from AI happen when companies limit themselves to implement the technology only, without making other changes to the business and the organization. Merely installing AI software in your company is not enough. Business executives must do much more than ask IT to do an AI project. This book describes seven points business leaders must address to receive the full benefits of

AI. AI is not an IT-only initiative.

This book applies Harvard, MIT studies, and other verified sources that prove how some companies have achieved new levels of competitiveness with artificial intelligence. The approach of this book is not technical; it focuses on what business leaders need to do to achieve greater competitiveness through artificial intelligence. Board members and company functions, including Information Technology, must work together to find new ways of doing business and serve customers through AI applications.

Companies using AI provide unparalleled customer experience, increasing sales, enhancing digital commerce, reducing cost, and preventing fraud. AI is taking these companies to unseen levels of competitiveness and profitability. By applying the seven points described in this book, your company can achieve similar success.

Today, artificial intelligence is the technology with the most significant potential for businesses. Companies in all industries are already starting to invest in AI. Now is the time to start using AI to grow the business. Delaying the AI initiative may mean competitors will get ahead. Act now.

What you will learn with this book

This book provides business executives with the knowledge to achieve new competitiveness levels by upgrading the organization. Upgrading the organization means moving to an omnichannel or ecosystem business model to profit from networks of customers, suppliers, and stakeholders, redesigning key processes to eliminate delay-causing bottlenecks, and addressing organizational culture. With his book, you will learn how to:

1. Use artificial intelligence profitably by improving customer experience, digital commerce, productivity, employee engagement, and marketing effectiveness while reducing cost and risk.
2. Identify AI opportunities and lead organizations to

implement them and obtain the benefits.

3. Compete with an updated digital business model to bring new revenues by connecting with others using AI technologies.
4. Implement AI with a detailed roadmap for executives.
5. Use the artificial intelligence age implications on businesses and everyday life by examining what successful companies do to excel now.
6. Apply proven 21st Century business practices leveraging digital networks to bring more revenues.
7. Explain how artificial intelligence is critical for companies of all sizes and convince business executives of the need to leverage AI.
8. Redesign processes to create frictionless interactions with clients.
9. Overcome the new challenges AI may bring, including security, ethics, and privacy.
10. Plan ways to profit from low energy, computing power, and telecommunications costs. Plan how to use the increasing data availability for AI applications.
11. Turn employee resistance to change to a culture open to change.
12. Distinguish among AI myths from facts and clear AI concepts for others.
13. Navigate the impact of AI on the creation, loss, and transformation of jobs.
14. Create a culture of data in the organization.
15. Use innovative tools and techniques to generate new ideas.

The promise of this book

Many business executives want AI to transform their business but are not sure how to apply it. Few people know what AI is, and fewer know how to implement it successfully in a company. This book explains the steps leaders must take on the business side to reap the rewards of AI. Leaders must link the AI initiatives to business value and move to a digital business model to achieve AI's full potential.

They must also remove non-value-added steps in critical processes and address organizational culture issues to manage employees' resistance to change. This book offers 65 AI examples to increase profitability you may use in your organization. In addition, the book includes a detailed, sequenced roadmap for AI implementation from the executive's perspective. Figure 1 shows the components of this book. This book is not technical. It is a business book on how to apply AI technology.

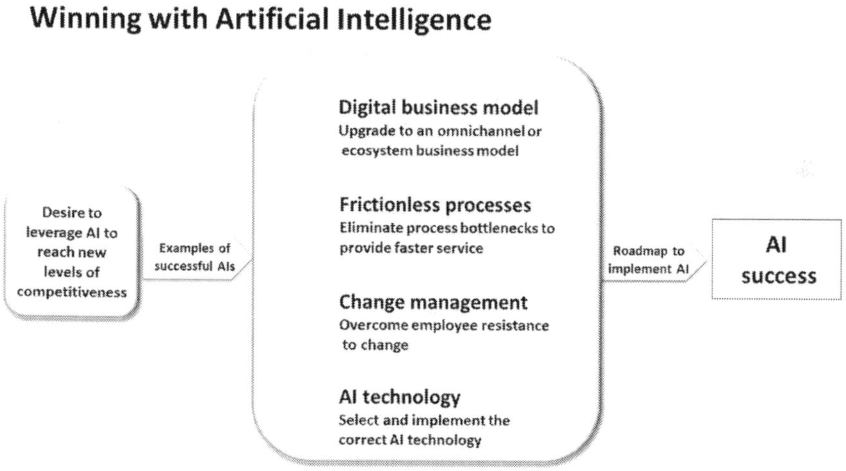

Winning with Artificial Intelligence

Digital business model
Upgrade to an omnichannel or ecosystem business model

Frictionless processes
Eliminate process bottlenecks to provide faster service

Change management
Overcome employee resistance to change

AI technology
Select and implement the correct AI technology

Desire to leverage AI to reach new levels of competitiveness

Examples of successful AIs

Roadmap to implement AI

AI success

Figure 1. Winning with artificial intelligence

This book will distinguish you as a leader capable of implementing artificial intelligence to achieve new competitive levels. We are still in the early days of AI use in business, and there are plenty of opportunities. In a recent survey by McKinsey, less than 25% of companies using AI had significantly impacted the bottom line[2]. Today is the correct time to embark on the AI journey to make your business more competitive. The reward for correctly implementing AI will be an unprecedented level of competitiveness.

This book shows how to use AI to achieve new levels of business competitiveness

Artificial intelligence technology works. What separates successful AI projects from those that fail are business, process, and organizational issues, not the technology's ability to accelerate the business. Many of the problems with AI are not due to the technology but to management's understanding of how the business must migrate to new digital business models, create smooth processes, and give customers a compelling value proposition. AI projects fail because of not blending the technology into the business and its culture[3]. Learning how to avoid these common mistakes will translate into higher profits. This book provides executives, managers, and business professionals in all functions with a competitive edge in using AI technology to compete in the new digital age.

Artificial intelligence, AI, is not only about technology; it is about change. It is not a question of *if* but of *when* and *how*. Given the disruption artificial intelligence will cause, addressing it is no longer a choice; it is a business imperative. AI can be a force for winning, taking the business to new profitability levels, but leaders must apply it with other business changes. Delaying AI now may mean the company will not survive.

Executives can no longer afford to have a poor understanding of how AI can propel businesses today. Ignoring AI or leaving it only to Information Technology would be a strategic error. The longer executives wait to implement AI, the more they will be left behind, and catching up later may not be possible. This book will show how to succeed with AI by approaching it with business, organization, process, culture, and technology viewpoints.

If you have asked yourself how to reach your strategic business goals with AI or achieve new productivity levels, this book is for you.

Now is the time to seize new opportunities. Continue to Chapter 1 to learn more.

Dr. Militza Basualdo

August 2021

AMAZING OPPORTUNITIES EVERYWHERE!

The world is changing because AI is widespread. Alexa, Siri, and chatbots are good examples of AI today, and many more are emerging. AI is poised to become the most disruptive technology over the coming years, and we will need to change the way we run businesses. What makes AI so powerful is its ability to learn. We cannot ignore that the digital and analog worlds are coming together[1]. This book makes sense of the way businesses must adapt to compete in this age.

AI is transforming all industries in an accelerated way. Digital technology is developing at an exponential rate. Even if artificial intelligence does not become superior to humans' capacity in our lifetimes, AI will enhance and change many of the operational tasks done today by humans. Many workers will either lose their jobs or see them transformed, but all industries will create new, higher-paying jobs. The opportunity to create companies is unprecedented in human history. The industrial revolution reshaped the economy, and AI is doing the same, except the impact will be evident at a fraction of the time[1].

Businesses need leaders capable of change to provide new ways of servicing customers, improving operations, and achieving new competitiveness with AI. To implement AI, we will continue to need data engineers, big data analysts, and other technical people, but, above all, we will need business leaders capable of changing the organization. Today's leaders must demystify AI concepts for executives, identify all the use cases, and focus on applying AI to increase customer value. The AI technology works; what we need now are people with ambition, vision, and energy to make the changes in the businesses.

AI is necessary for businesses to reap the rewards of digital transformation. The digital transformation initiatives are not over yet, and AI's total development is far from reaching its inflection point. AI should not be ignored or underestimated. AI experts and professionals have described the potential impact of AI on businesses equivalent to the internet's wide adoption. AI can deliver an additional US 13 trillion by 2030, or about 1.2% additional GDP growth per year[2].

The future is accelerating

A wonderful world is emerging. The exponential development of new technologies and the increasing automation levels are giving way to a world very different from the past but full of new possibilities, even one filled with abundance. By 2026, half of the world's population will finally have an internet connection, adding four billion fresh minds with access to information and communication. New ideas will no longer just come from Silicon Valley; the entire world will discover, invent, and create new ideas and businesses. Can you imagine what four billion minds with information and connectivity do for humanity? In the past, we had many geniuses whose talents went unused simply because they lived and died in remote villages, never having access to information resources. As the world gets connected, more people will have the ability to make their ideas work for others[3].

The cost of everything from computing to storage is dropping very fast, opening new opportunities. Once something becomes digital, its development becomes exponential, as was the case with the human genome and solar technologies. Here are some facts:

- The cost of energy will drop; the sun already gives us 6,000 times the power we need. We are not far from paying a penny per kilowatt-hour from the sun[4].
- Abundant energy means abundant water.
- From 1993 to 2015, we saw a million times increase in computation power for the same cost. The prices for bandwidth and storage are plummeting.
- In the next ten years, all industries will need to transform,

and 40% of current companies will cease to exist.
- Crowdfunding has made it easier to try new business ideas.
- Over the last 100 years, the cost of energy dropped a hundred-fold, the cost of transportation dropped a thousand-fold, and telecommunications' price decreased by a million-fold over the last 100 years (Diamandis, 2019). Phone calls between different countries used to cost dollars per minute—now, there are multiple ways to make those calls for free.
- The cost of sequencing a human genome was initially $2.7 billion. Now the price is below $1,000 and will soon be $100.
- The number of sensors connected to the internet will increase by 100 times in the next ten years. According to McKinsey, the sensors and the internet of things may create a new economic value of $6.2 trillion. We will be able to know anything at any time and anywhere. Soon what will matter is not what you know but the questions you ask.
- Netflix killed Blockbuster, and none of the large music companies invented MP3. The disruptors generally come from outside the company. Approximately 25% of disruptions come from outside the industry. Between 25% and 50% of the disruptors will be new companies.
- More wealth will be created in the next ten years than in the last 100 years[4].

The dropping cost of technology and commodities changes the way we plan. When technologies are accelerating at exponential speed, linear thinking will fall short. Strategic plans must incorporate these new premises, and these situations open new doors not previously seen in the history of humankind.

Definition of artificial intelligence

Artificial intelligence, AI, is the computer science branch that simulates human intelligence[5]. A critical difference between traditional applications and AI is that AI can learn from data, whereas applications can only execute code. AI automates tasks that require human intelligence[6]. AI applications are not the traditional programs whose logic provided for all the foreseen situations that could happen. AI continues to learn even after it is running. AI is not about imitating humans as it is about transforming how businesses compete and operate[1].

John McCarthy, known as the father of artificial intelligence, coined the phrase "artificial intelligence" in 1956[3]. Artificial intelligence was popular in the 1950s and 1960s, applying computer vision technologies. When this technology failed to produce results, the enthusiasm for AI ceased. Artificial intelligence went through a winter in the 1970s, 1980s, and 1990s mainly due to a lack of computing power and data[3]. In the 1980s and 1990s, machine learning was added to artificial intelligence, although the results were modest. It was not until 2012 that artificial intelligence took off when deep learning or deep neural networks arrived. By then, we already had enough data computing power and data to feed and process artificial intelligence.

There are three primary levels of artificial intelligence:

1. Weak or narrow AI can perform only a limited number of tasks based on learning from massive amounts of data. Today, we have weak AI.
2. Strong AI capable of having consciousness and self-awareness to make decisions at the human level. Scientists are still debating when AI will reach this point. Consciousness and self-awareness may be necessary for AI to equal human level because many decisions people make are based on emotions.
3. Superior AI possesses an intelligence superior to human beings, controlling its existence.

We do not need to worry about strong or superior AI's as they are far away in the future. AI can sense, think and act, as shown in figure 2. AI is not a single technology but an umbrella of technologies that includes machine learning, deep learning, natural language processing, speech recognition, robotics, expert systems, computer vision, algorithms, and text processing.

Artificial Intelligence can . . .

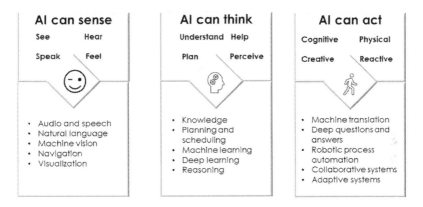

Figure 2. AI can sense, think and act

When combined with process automation tools, AI can:

- Reduce repetitive manual tasks to increase productivity, lower costs and allow the staff to focus on higher-value activities.
- Generate insights from data to facilitate operations, identify trends and personalize service.

Just as important as knowing what AI can do, the current narrow AI cannot reason. To avoid using the wrong results due to partial data or flawed processing, leaders should understand the business value AI will deliver[7].

AI can have different meanings to each person. The AI-related terms must be clearly defined and communicated to all to avoid frustration and lack of support for AI.

11

Why is AI critical to companies?

AI changes the way computers help businesses. AI algorithms can learn by themselves 24 hours a day without resting like us. The knowledge AI accumulates makes it capable of giving companies new perspectives and ideas to manage the business in new ways. This new approach allows companies to achieve higher competitiveness, higher margins, and enhanced digital commerce, among other benefits. Many leaders have realized that AI makes the company agile, innovative, and able to scale. AI is transformative by nature, and companies who have not adopted it may already be years behind competitors. Additional delays in implementing AI may damage the competitiveness of the business. A significant difference between AI and traditional systems is that AI will make decisions after learning and analyzing the data. In contrast, conventional systems present the data and leave the decision-making to humans.

Enhancing the customer experience is the most common reason to implement AI, with over half of the corporations basing their justification of AI on this point. AI uses natural language processing to spot data patterns to detect a customer's mood and take the appropriate action. For example, AI can learn by observing customers' viewing and buying behavior to identify what they are looking for and when they open to making a purchase. AI can also specify the best time to send promotional materials to customers to increase the probability of being read. AI can even draft attractive messages based on its knowledge of customers who have not transacted with the company to entice them to return. Finally, AI can predict when corrective maintenance will be needed and anticipate customers' needs.

AI is not just for large businesses. AI is available today, and organizations of all sizes can implement it. A common myth is that AI may only be justifiable in Fortune 500 companies. AI may be purchased as part of a packaged software or even paid as a subscription, making it not only affordable but simple to implement without the need for high-level specialists[8]. Unless the AI application aims to provide a unique competitive advantage, companies should seek packaged AI first. AI experts are not abundant, but this situation need not deter companies. If the application the company has in mind is not available as a package, they can use crowdsourcing or outsourcing it, tapping on AI talent worldwide. There is no need to make significant investments in infrastructure or talent to start using AI. To compete in the future, AI will not be optional for companies regardless of size.

How to convince the business to use AI

Artificial intelligence is not an island. Most AI implementations will require the involvement and cooperation of multiple areas[9]. For example, a Finance project will need support from Legal, Security, Technology, Compliance, and Human Resources. In addition, to succeed with AI executives, back-office managers, and frontline employees will need to cooperate. These steps help to gain the support of the organization.

Obtain upper management support
Multiple formal studies point to the need to have management support for any significant change initiative, artificial intelligence included. Some of the members of upper management may still hesitate to use technology. Yet, without their support, artificial intelligence in a business will probably not be successful. Senior management does not need to understand AI's technical aspects, but they need a practical understanding of how the company can compete in new ways. Artificial intelligence frequently appears in social media, so executives must differentiate between myths and reality.

Focus on the company's key objectives. Any major project must contribute to the company's key objectives for leaders to perceive any value. Company executives regard projects that do not contribute to the central business goals the same or even worse than not doing anything. Many project teams have worked very hard in the past only to find that their leaders considered they wasted their time and resources. AI is not different in this respect. Focusing on the key company goals first, identifying an AI project that will significantly contribute to it, and showing the leaders this potential, will increase the executive's acceptance of AI.

Highlight revenue potential. Appeal to business leaders by pointing to how AI has the potential to increase the bottom line. AI can reduce cost, increase productivity, and improve profits to grow[9]. AI will impact all industries in all its functions and boost profitability by as much as 20%.

Stay ahead of the competition. The fear of missing out, FOMO, is a powerful motivator. If the business leaders do not act now, they are running the risk of falling behind. Failure to invest in AI's organizational and technical aspects may mean project failure and inability to compete in the future. If a company delays the decision to adopt new technology runs the danger of the competition being so advanced, it will take too long for the business to catch up.

Do a pilot project, show the results. Pick a small project to prove AI can deliver results. Leaders often need to see tangible results in their organization to believe in technology. Therefore, pick a project that can be concluded in a short time and does not depend on other projects that may delay it. For example, if the AI pilot is a chatbot dealing with customer support inquiries, pick a small portion, 20% to 30%, of the most common questions and gradually expand as the chatbot learns to answer other questions[9].

Always emphasize the value of the business instead of the technology to be used. Keep expectations low. Refer to the business value potential, avoid focusing on the technology itself. Executives and managers using AI will replace executives and managers without AI.

Ten myths (and facts) about AI

Artificial intelligence is still a buzzword conjuring images from replacing one's brain with a technology that will take us to the

Jetsons world. The AI initiative could fail if everyone has different ideas of artificial intelligence. An excellent way to achieve a common understanding of AI is to clarify its myths. Here are the most common myths that exist and the facts to refute them:

Myth 1 - AI will take over all the jobs.
Reality - AI will change existing jobs and create new ones.

Machines and algorithms will create 133 million new jobs and eliminate 75 million jobs leaving a net gain of 58 million jobs[10]. However, few jobs will remain the same. Most employees will need to upskill to work with AI. For example, chatbots are now using sentiment analysis to route the calls where a human must deal with an angry customer with a higher level of emotional engagement. As the technologies continue to evolve, business complexity will also increase, resulting in an increased need for human judgment[11].

Myth 2 - AI needs highly trained specialists and large budgets.
Reality - You can buy or rent AI without specialists.

Many AI tools are already available, so data scientists and machine learning experts are not always needed. Many companies are buying, and even renting, applications equipped with AI. For example, Alexa's code was re-applied in business applications needing speaker-independent voice recognition and noise-canceling[11]. Training a chatbot usually requires the same information used to train call center associates.

Myth 3 - AI can learn from any set of data, even messy data.
Reality - AI needs clean data.

Garbage in, garbage out. AI learns from its input data. If the datasets feeding the AI used to screen resumes consist only of tall persons, the result would be that AI will eliminate short persons as potential candidates for the job. AI needs information that has been curated and is of high quality[11].

Myth 4 - AI works just like a human brain.
Reality - AI is a technology, not a human.

AI simulates several tasks humans perform, but AI is not human, and we are still far from reaching that point. Instead, AI works according to the data it receives. Humans define the scenarios and cases where AI will operate, but AI cannot define new instances. An AI at the same level as human intelligence is called artificial general intelligence, and experts disagree when it happens[11].

Myth 4 – Artificial intelligence and machine learning are the same.
Reality - Machine learning is part of artificial intelligence.
Machine learning feeds large quantities of data to the application for training the AI solution. Machine learning needs an unbiased set of clean data and a data acquisition strategy. AI encompasses multiple techniques ranging from natural language processing to expert systems[12].

Myth 5 – AI can learn on its own.
Reality - No, AI needs to be fed.
AI may appear to learn independently, but human data scientists must define the problem, prepare the data, clean the data, remove biases, and update the feeding cycle[12]. Many businesses and processes were affected when the COVID-19 pandemic hit. The existing AI had to be fed new data because life had changed, but AI had no way of knowing.

Myth 6 – AI is not biased.
Reality - AIs are biased only if they are fed biased data.
Humans are biased in some form, even if some biases are positive such as commitment and loyalty. AI is a technology that receives data and rules from humans and, as such, is prone to human biases, both positive and negative. AI systems must continue to learn to keep abreast of the current conditions. To ensure AI only receives unbiased data, the teams selecting the data should have diversity and have other groups review the data[12].

Myth 7 – My company does not need an AI strategy.
Reality - Yes, you do.
AI is a powerful technology that gives businesses new ways to compete and grow, and companies must investigate how to apply it to meet their goals. AI is an immediate problem solver and a

strategic way to augment decisions. In the next four years, 69% of work done by managers will be automated[12]. Companies would do well to consider AI to fulfill their strategies. Failure to consider AI in a business could place it at a significant competitive disadvantage.

Myth 8 – I don't trust AI.
Reality – AI is more transparent now.
AI has been perceived as a "black box" in the past, and even today, some AI applications are still opaque. Software providers have an enormous pressure to make the AI results transparent, especially where human lives or millions of dollars are involved. Banks, hospitals, and most industries will not work with black boxes[13]. AI needs to provide sufficient transparency without overwhelming users to gain their understanding.

Myth 9– AI cannot be creative.
Reality – AI can be creative.
With the correct human understanding and intuition, AI can produce paintings, articles, music, and even new cooking recipes. AI is not a famous artist yet, but it already creates new works never seen by humans.

Myth 10 – It's going to kill us.
Reality – No
AI works according to the data and rules humans feed it. Humans dominate the earth. AI will only do what humans request. We need to be careful about the goals we set for AI to accomplish and the restrictions we provide. AI will find ways to reach the objectives, and we do not want to be standing blocking the goal. We must apply the three rules Isaac Asimov defined for robots many years ago.

1. A robot may not injure a human being.
2. A robot must obey humans unless it violates the first rule.
3. A robot must self-preserve unless this protection conflicts with the previous two rules.

Many artificial intelligence myths are a byproduct of science fiction. We should not believe these myths, but we must be aware of them to dispel them promptly if they come up in the organization. Executives must have the correct expectations of AI, or the AI initiative will fail when unrealistic results are anticipated, wasting precious time as competitors advance in its use. Workers armed with AI and related technologies are already here. Now the job is to bring AI augmentation to the next level[11].

How AI evolved

AI technologies, computer processing speed, and massive data availability have been evolving since the 1950s. In 2012, a breakthrough was achieved with the development of deep learning, a new way for computers to learn and reach their conclusions. The new AI technology opened new opportunities for businesses to use AI. Learning by themselves, machines can produce novel ideas that humans have not imagined. Here is a brief AI history, a description of the present, and probable developments in the future.

Past

In the imagination of humanity, artificial intelligence has been alive for centuries. Artificial intelligence first appeared as part of Greek mythology as robot-like beings. In 1818, when Mary Shelley published the book Frankenstein, people began to fear a machine created by humans that could kill other humans. During the first half of the 20th Century, movies such as The Wizard of Oz portrayed robots without hearts[14]. Artificial intelligence as a scientific field arrived during the 1950s:

- 1956: The term "artificial intelligence" started in 1956[8].
- 1950s – 1974: Computer vision made some progress.
- 1974: Over-optimistic AI goals and lack of computer processing capacity and data killed the enthusiasm for AI.
- 1974 – 1980: First AI winter.
- 1980 – 1987: Expert systems, computer applications emulating an expert's decision-making process, surged as a form of AI.
- 1987 - 1993: Second AI winter.

- 1990s: Machine learning was introduced. Machine learning is a part of artificial intelligence where persons train machines to recognize patterns based on data and make predictions.
- 1997: Using machine learning, IBM's Deep Blue defeated chess champion Garry Kasparov
- 2011: IBM's Watson computer wins against human contestants at Jeopardy!
- 2012: Deep learning, the most advanced part of machine learning, was developed. With deep learning, the machine can learn on its own, reason, and obtain its conclusions. Deep learning came at the appropriate time when computing power had become powerful enough, and the data necessary for AI to learn was available.
- 2013: Advances in neural networks help attract billions of dollars in AI investment from leading technology companies.
- 2016: Google's AlphaGo beat top-ranked player Lee Se-dol[15].

Present

Many persons still think artificial intelligence is a technology for the future. Today, artificial intelligence is already present in daily life. Here are some examples:

- Email filter to eliminate spam messages and show only the emails of interest to the person. In many of today's email systems, artificial intelligence learns from the user to classify each message more accurately. For example, a daily email from a particular source is classified as "promotional" first, but it will soon appear in the inbox if the user clicks on it every day.
- When the user writes an email, the system will often suggest the rest of the sentence saving work. For example, if a user types "When would it be convenient for us," the system may indicate the text "to meet?"
- Smart speakers such as Alexa, Siri, or Cortana answer our questions and perform tasks for us.
- Intelligent search engines to find the information we are

looking for from the universe of the internet. Can you imagine life without Google?

- Amazon recommends other items we may like.
- Movies we may like as recommended by Netflix.
- Translators from one language to another have recently improved due to AI. Robots use translation of voice to text and text to voice when conversing with people.
- Hedge funds are using AI to beat the stock market.
- Improved hearing aids eliminate noise with AI.
- Glasses for the elderly can adjust according to the vision's degeneration due to age.
- Robots can prepare food and coffee[16].

Future

AI in its present form is still very limited. AI can learn to do one thing and become better at doing that one thing, but it cannot do anything else. That is the reason experts refer to the current AI as weak or narrow AI.

Emotional AIs. Philosophers and scientists are already debating whether AI should have emotions. If AI will one day reach human intelligence, it will need some degree of emotion because humans, whether we like it or not, make some of our decisions using our feelings. No emotions would mean AI applications resemble Mr. Spock from Star Trek.

AIs with consciousnesses. Another area of discussion among scientists is whether AI should have consciousness. Consciousness is being aware of one's body and environment, while self-awareness recognizes that consciousness, being aware of one's existence[17]. A human infant is conscious of its surroundings but is not yet self-aware. In the first years of life, children become aware of who they are and recognize themselves in the mirror. What AI with consciousness will look like is akin to asking what it feels like to be a Tesla. We do not know.

Scientists converge on the idea that AI will one day have consciousness. The theory of the mind states that decisions are affected by the person's beliefs, desires, and intentions. These beliefs, desires, preferences, and perspectives may differ from our own[5]. In the future, machines with self-awareness will understand their feelings and speculate the feelings of others.

AI intelligence reaching human-level intelligence. The final goal of AI is artificial general intelligence, a self-teaching system that can outperform humans across all disciplines; in other words, computers as intelligent as people[18]. Many experts are arguing if this will happen in 20 years or centuries from now. The Future of Humanity Institute at Oxford University interviewed 352 AI researchers on how they viewed AI's future. The study found that AI will likely progress to outperform humans according to this timeline:

- Translating languages by 2024
- Writing high school essays by 2026
- Driving trucks by 2027
- Working in retail by 2031
- Writing best-selling books by 2049
- Performing surgeries by 2053

The closer the year of prediction, the higher the chance of being correct. The study found a 50% chance of AI outperforming humans in all tasks in 45 years and automating all human jobs in 120 years[19]. When AI starts to outperform humans in basic, repetitive tasks, humanity will focus on more creative jobs.

Computers reaching human-level intelligence is called Singularity. When Singularity happens, the computers will not stop but will continue to evolve, exceeding human intelligence by many folds at an accelerated pace. What happens next is more appropriate for science fiction than for this book.

Regulations for AI. The world will change drastically because of AI, and new rules will be required. For example, today's sensors in self-driving cars detect persons with lighter skin tones better than dark-skinned people. The reason is that AI learned from pictures of persons with light skin color. New requirements standards for training and testing AI need to be developed[20]. The issue of regulated AI is not trivial. Deep learning used by AI is essentially a black box not easily audited. For use cases, such as how Facebook identifies who to tag in each picture, no explanation is needed. On the other hand, for AI systems diagnosing skin cancer, understanding how AI concluded may be a matter of life or death[20].

Will AI eliminate jobs?

Much hype talks about AI taking over tasks and eliminating jobs. AI is changing the nature of work and even the business model. AI-based machines can perform some tasks faster than humans, complement humans in their work, and complete tasks humans cannot do. The result is that some jobs will be eliminated while new jobs will be created. Companies have been using AI since 2013, and so far, more jobs have been added than eliminated. The net effect is that many jobs have changed. The elimination of current jobs and the creation of employment is not new; history has plenty of examples:

Photographs replaced paintings. More than a century ago, the invention of photography put many painters out of work[1]. Instead of artists painting portraits, new stores opened selling cameras, film, and other accessories. Film processing became an industry. The photographic sector suffered another major shift when the 21st Century arrived, and digital cameras became popular. The photography industry diminished, but now everyone has a camera in their pocket. Film processing was no longer necessary, but the demand for extra storage to store digital pictures surged. People started taking many more photos than before, giving way to new types of companies such as Facebook and TikTok[1]. In the end, smartphones killed Kodak.

Cars replaced horse-led buggies. Blacksmiths stopped making horseshoes and started to work with metals in car factories. Horse stable workers lost their jobs as the horse population decreased. In exchange, new jobs were created, such as auto mechanics, gas station attendants, car parts shops, car assembly workers, and car salespersons, among others. Horse buggies disappeared, but a much more robust automotive industry came into being. The transition from horses to cars happened within a decade. In 1907, there were 140,000 cars in the US. By 1917, the number of vehicles had a 33-fold increase to almost five million[21].

Automatic switchboards replaced telephone operators. For over a Century, telephone operators would connect calls by manually inserting plugs into the correct jacks. At its peak in the United States, 100,000 people worked as telephone operators. The new switchboards eliminated most of these jobs in the 1960s. Today only a few operators remain, mainly for emergency cases.

Word processing and voice mail eliminated secretaries. When word processing and voice mail arrived, corporations had less need for secretaries. Organizations re-arranged their structures so that instead of executives having their secretary, a pool of assistants would serve the entire department. Many secretarial positions were eliminated, and others moved to new jobs.

The internet creates new jobs. When the use of the internet became widespread, the concern over job loss became prevalent. Indeed, jobs such as travel agents, postmasters, file clerks, librarians, and newspaper deliverers are no longer as plentiful as they were in 1990. In exchange for these jobs, we now have web developers, community managers, user experience designers, SEO consultants, and cloud services specialists, among others.

New technologies transform the nature of the work and can perform more tasks than humans[8]. The result is that some jobs will decline while others will grow. In the automobile, internet, and now the mobile revolutions, far more jobs have been created than eliminated[9]. The jobs created were higher paying than the ones made obsolete, but people needed new training. Effective managers will make employees aware of the training they will need and facilitate the training resources. Millions of employees will need new skills because of AI. Some technical skills will be required, but soft skills such as creativity, communication, and critical thinking will be necessary[22]. The mentality to continue acquiring new skills will continue beyond AI. With the rapid pace of new technologies, an interest in life-long learning is critical for all persons who wish to remain productive.

Artificial intelligence and other emerging technologies will change most jobs. All workers will need to acquire new skills to remain employable. Repetitive and dull jobs will probably disappear soon. Each job consists of related tasks. Automation will replace tasks, not jobs. Routine tasks are easy to program. Non-routine tasks such as those that require creativity or solving complex problems will be more difficult to automate[6]. As AI learns to perform duties, the applications will create new tasks, but we still need to wait to see how these new tasks will form the future jobs[6].

Many large companies employ mid-level managers who keep track of other people's routine tasks. Intelligent machines will replace these jobs with AI's, who may even show more empathy than the current human managers. Smart devices have more time to spend with each employee and can assimilate much of each person's hopes, ambitions, and needs. Today's developers are already working on solutions to create computers capable of expressing empathy, sympathy, caring, and even humor and respond appropriately to these emotions[16]. The computers will be expressing emotions but not feeling them. The middle managers who remain will be responsible for designing and executing AI-driven processes with less emphasis on supervising human employees. Human managers will be better at coaching and promoting a work culture, but AIs will be better at providing unbiased information, maintaining work schedules, and problem-solving. An advantage these machines will have over humans is that they will not burst into anger or impatience.

Managers need to shuffle positions when part of the task goes to a machine, and the other part continues under human care. A recent study done by the MIT-IBM Watson AI Lab analyzed 170 million online job posts between 2010 and 2017. The results of the study showed that occupations change slowly, but tasks are frequently re-arranged. Employee compensation will need to change to reflect the value of the new work done by employees working with AI[22].

Knowledge will overtake experience. Many leaders are proud of the experience and knowledge they have accumulated over their work lives. This knowledge was precious during the 20th Century, but AI and analytics produce new perspectives on many aspects of the business, making the knowledge acquired through experience quickly become obsolete. Influential leaders need to let go of much of what they know and be willing to learn new ideas. Old ways do not open new doors. Global connectivity means that leaders may have to accept contributions from employees and external resources at all levels[23].

How to prepare for AI, skills needed

AI will impact all future jobs. Computers will eventually outperform humans not by copying us but by processing vast quantities of data with AI applications to reach new ways to understand situations. At least half of all employees will need new skills over the next few years[24]. Everyone needs to be aware of the skills that will be required soon. AI is strong at digesting data to formulate new perspectives, but AI is still weak in soft skills where people excel. The skills people will need to complement the latest technologies are creativity, caring for people, critical thinking, and emotional intelligence. Given the acceleration of change, everyone will need increased self-management to adapt to the new circumstances by learning, tolerating stress, and staying flexible[24]. Learning to learn is necessary to remain relevant and employable.

All of us need to increase our data literacy. Data is the fuel behind today's disruptions. Companies have massive data, but data by itself is worthless. Leaders will need to learn to use data effectively and extract insights to make better decisions. Perhaps the skill highest in demand is tech-savviness. Today, we have many emerging technologies that individually would transform businesses but together are reshaping all industries. We now have artificial intelligence, 3D printing, robotics, blockchain, the internet of things, and virtual reality interacting with each other to change the world. Managers need to understand the changes, how fast these technologies are developing, and their impact on the business.

Some persons worry about jobs leaving for other countries, but technology will make many current jobs obsolete. With sufficient training, workers will leave their disappearing jobs for new, higher-paying employment.

How this book will help

The purpose of this book is to give business leaders a working understanding of how to reach new competitiveness levels by changing the business model, processes and opening the organization to the change, leveraging the use of AI. This book is not technical. It is a book about improving business results with artificial intelligence. The book differs from others because it provides executives with a step-by-step roadmap to implement AI and collect its rewards. Business leaders who can upgrade business practices through AI will become valuable players in any enterprise.

This book consists of five chapters; each chapter builds on the previous ones. Chapter 1, "Amazing opportunities everywhere!", offered a view of the massive changes happening in this world, basic AI concepts, why AI is critical to businesses, and how to convince an organization of AI's benefits. The new business vision must be developed incorporating the disruptive changes coming shortly.

Chapter 2, "Upgrading the company to the 21st Century," first examines life in the age of AI as the background to introduce the changes businesses need to make to use AI well. The chapter

26

describes the AI age and the framework for upgrading a company to the 21st Century. This framework consists of three parts. The first part is to prepare the organization for AI by acquiring data and getting acquainted with AI. The second part of the framework is enhancing the company's operations with smooth processes. The third part of the framework is to move to a digital business model. Today, most companies still operate in a traditional business model, but moving up to an omnichannel or ecosystem business model will give better service to customers and improve profitability.

Chapter 3, "65 profitable ways to use AI", describes the primary uses of artificial intelligence and its benefits to spark new ideas. AI offers use successful cases in all industries and across all functions. Leaders may pick the ideas that best contribute to their core strategies.

Chapter 4, "AI implementation roadmap for executives," presents a detailed roadmap to implement AI in any organization. This chapter describes a four-phase roadmap for implementing AI and the specific steps in each phase. The four stages of the roadmap are understanding AI, preparing for AI, implementing AI, and reaping the benefits. This roadmap guides executives in preparing the organization to amplify the benefits of AI. The roadmap is not technical.

Chapter 5, "Winning with AI: A summary," summarizes the previous chapters' learnings. The book concludes by describing the new responsibilities and opportunities leaders have in the AI era.

Your successful future with AI

Business executives must first understand artificial intelligence, its benefits, risks, and interaction with the business[25]. The decision to compete using AI must change how the business operates to achieve AIs full potential. Knowing the strengths and limitations of each business model will permit leaders to build AI applications to give customers new experiences.

The use of AI has had a meteorite development over the last

decade. AI offers new ways to increase sales addressing customer needs with the power of technology. Business leaders who genuinely understand the nature of the business models powered by AI will be the ones who achieve the most significant competitiveness levels for their businesses.

UPGRADING THE COMPANY
TO THE 21ST CENTURY

Imagine needing a bank loan. Instead of dressing up, driving to the branch, and waiting in line to talk with an officer to request the loan, you log to the bank's website and input all the information. Within a second of hitting enter, the website tells you the bank approved the request for the loan. You check your balance and see the bank has already transferred the money you requested. Sounds far-fetched? Ant Group is already doing this for its billion customers throughout the world[1].

Artificial intelligence, AI, has changed the marketplace. Businesses using AI are transforming the way they serve customers by differentiating their services. With AI, organizations can perform transactions without human intervention at a fraction of the time and cost. Computers are now doing the work that humans previously did, only faster and with new insights. For example, Amazon's AI can calculate and change the prices of each item every second, if necessary, a feat that not even a large team of persons could do accurately. When AI-driven computers manage a company's everyday transactions, firms find that they quickly scale up to handle larger volumes without hiring additional employees.

This chapter is critical because it describes how companies can be competitive in today's AI era. The chapter starts with a brief description of the current environment, followed by the framework to transform a business into a 21st Century company. This framework consists of three steps: enable an AI-ready, optimize core processes, and upgrade the business model, while implementing AI and other emerging technologies.

Living in the age of AI

In many ways, today's age is profoundly different from the way we lived, even a few years ago. Customers' expectations, competitors' tactics, technology innovation, and the economic environment have changed. The changes in customer expectations drive businesses to analyze the massive information obtained through applications, social media, and other sources to create a personalized, digital customer experience. Many companies are already using new technologies to serve customers. The rapid development of technology provides unique opportunities to learn more about the customer and make innovations. The AI age also has a darker side, enabling increased wealth inequality and information security risks.

Customers' expectations changed. Customers have always wanted a friendly and efficient service, but customers raised their expectations when the new technology arrived. Customers who have shopped at Amazon now demand everywhere else the same service Amazon provides. Customers like Amazon's personalized service, wide assortment, access to reviews, and easy ways to pay without leaving home. They also want free shipping and next-day delivery. People are now more empowered as customers. If they receive poor service or an inferior product, they can easily complain to hundreds of their social media contacts.

Social media is changing the definition of fast. After posting on social media, users invariably return a few minutes later to see how many "likes" or comments they received. Customers have become used to instant gratification and are now expecting the same response from businesses. If a customer asks about a product or service, most expect an answer within minutes, if not seconds.

Competitors have embraced new technologies. Over half of US corporations have already moved beyond designing their digital transformation and are exploring emerging technologies. The pandemic forced many businesses to offer customers new alternatives for shopping and interacting. In this process, businesses adopted new technologies. As consumers become more comfortable with technology, companies are rushing to satisfy new expectations.

Using data every day. Virtually everyone has a smartphone at hand with access to all the knowledge. Consumers can Google the product or service and compare characteristics and prices. Consumers who have problems with a product are more willing to look up information and resolve the issue themselves instead of dealing with unknowledgeable salespersons. Companies can decide to provide information online to reduce the number of calls customer service receives according to their customers' new habits.

Over 90% of the data we have today was created in the last two years. The massive amounts of data have resulted in new concepts such as data science, analytics, big data, and algorithms. During the 20th Century, companies used vertical integration to compete. With vertical integration, a business owns or controls its suppliers, distributors, or stores. The results are cost reduction, improved efficiencies, and process control. Today, many successful platform-based businesses such as Twitter, Facebook, Uber, or Airbnb do not use the traditional model. Companies with conventional stores started selling more online than in physical stores as COVID-19 changed buying habits. To win in today's world has less to do with traditional industry specialization and more with a set of capabilities such as data sourcing, processing, analytics, algorithm development, business model design, and AI to operate and make decisions[1]. Many newer companies use drivers such as network and learning effects instead of conventional expertise. The new focus has permeated new companies in their operation and hiring practices. When Uber hired a new CEO, they looked for someone with experience running a digital company (in this case, Expedia) rather than a transportation services executive[1].

Pervasive social media. It is hard to be in a restaurant, airport, or mall without seeing people bending over the cell phones checking their social media updates. Social media provides the platform for unregulated content sharing. For many people, the day's first and last activities are checking up on Facebook or Twitter. The use of social media is no longer limited to keeping up with friends. Businesses are using social media to increase brand awareness, generate leads, boost sales, manage their reputation, learn about their customers, keep an eye on competitors, and gauge customer sentiment for the brand, among others. Social media also has a darker side as some fake news now spreads faster.

Growing interconnectedness. Companies are thriving with increased business interconnectedness. LinkedIn, Amazon, and Twitter, among others, see their business grow through more connections. With increased interconnections, industry boundaries are disappearing. The emerging use of digitization is now connecting industries in new ways. Google entered the auto industry, and Alibaba established a bank thanks to digital interfaces. As data and analytics are evolving in one business, the insights and information are helpful in other industries. For example, Alibaba already had its customers' data and purchasing history and could easily transition to converting its customers to the bank's new customers. The higher the number of interconnections, the faster the exchange of ideas and the pace of innovation. Interconnections are essential to solve world problems such as climate change and detect pandemics early. Connections are increasing, and face-to-face interactions are declining.

New technologies. Technologies continue to evolve. Emerging technologies such as AI, the internet of things, blockchain, augmented reality, virtual reality, 5G, and distributed cloud are already used to run companies and serve customers. The combined use of these technologies is revolutionizing *all* industries. Each technology is powerful, but business disruption occurs when two or more technologies are used jointly.

Accelerated innovation. AI is transforming all industries at an accelerated pace. In the US, for example, it took over 50 years for

80% of the homes to have a landline telephone, but Americans adopted the smartphone in less than five years. The industrial revolution reshaped the economy, and AI is doing the same, except the impact will be evident at a fraction of the time[1].

The future success of businesses depends on their ability to innovate. Innovation is vital because it enables companies to penetrate markets faster. Transformative companies grow faster and are more profitable than traditional companies. Innovation is introducing something new that adds value and is the way companies stay relevant in a changing market. As new technologies emerge, companies must figure out how to serve customers better and find new ways to compete in the marketplace through these technologies. Most innovations fail to give results, but the few that work give huge advantages. Companies who prefer to avoid innovating and continue with the same operation will become irrelevant and gradually die.

Software runs companies. AI is accelerating businesses' operations at record speeds. Even today's weak AI is sufficient to transform the nature of business and change the way it operates. AI, analytics, and software are already running supply chain planning, warehouse management, capacity planning, qualifying a customer for a loan, setting prices, recommending products, handling customer inquiries, and even perform some Human Resources functions. During the 20th Century, humans instructed computers on what they should do. Computers today define what humans should do, such as finding the best path to find a specific product in a warehouse. When a business operates with AI software, algorithms become the way the company delivers value[1]. AI is now the engine of execution of the fastest-growing companies.

Personalized learning. The way we learn has changed. During the 20th Century, students had to sit on a hard chair and listen to teachers talk for hours. Some teachers were inspiring, but others surpassed the effects of a sleeping pill. The teacher gave everyone in the class the same lecture regardless of the learning preferences of each student. AI can now identify the type of preferred learning for each student from the first lesson. It modifies the following lessons' teaching techniques adapting to each student's style to maximize their learning. Experts have identified seven learning styles, verbal, visual, musical, physical, social, logical, and solitary. Each student has one or more types of learning styles with which they learn the fastest. A gifted teacher in an ideal setting with only one student perceives the student's preferred way of learning and adapts to it to learn quickly. If the same teacher has two students, the task of adapting to each one becomes more difficult. Adaptive learning can teach each student in a group in an individualized way.

Managers' work changes. Managers traditionally supervised a group of persons. As artificial intelligence takes over many of the tasks previously done by employees, managers must design, monitor, and run AI-based processes. As artificial intelligence continues to learn, machines become more intelligent over time and help managers with decision-making. AI could become an experienced mentor always available for advice and analysis. Today, many managers must make decisions with little data and spend much of their time managing routine tasks. With AI's predictive capabilities to make critical decisions and manage daily operations, managers will have more time for strategic tasks.

Life-long learning. Businesses are undergoing accelerated changes and need their workforce to upskill continuously to continue being relevant and productive. Online classes allow employees to keep up with new developments while meeting job, family, and social responsibilities. Digital academic libraries offer the world's knowledge at our fingertips. Video tutorials and sites such as Coursera, YouTube, and Udemy offer concise training on many topics at the time and pace we want. Blogs can teach us many subjects. With so many resources, anybody can continue to learn. For the coming years, the outlook for education is that formal multiyear programs may be outdated by the time the student graduates. Shorter courses at the time the skills are needed will be more in demand.

Not everything is rosy in the AI age. The AI age has some downsides, wealth inequality, and increased risks in cybersecurity. Wealth in the hands of a few has been a source of jealousy and wars throughout human history. With digital businesses, wealth inequality will grow even more. The high-speed flow of transactions and data into digital networks has increased power and value[1]. As the digital networks continue to carry more transactions, companies such as Amazon, Google, and Alibaba are growing faster than traditional companies. Businesses can more easily enter new businesses, such as Alibaba, by leveraging the vast information they already have[1].

A major problem today is the increased frequency and intensity of cyberattacks. More data means more wealth but also the risk of someone trying to steal it. Attacks on information have become more common, and information security leaders cannot discover them fast enough. The malware may be present for months transferring critical data to the attackers' servers before being discovered.

Framework for moving the company to the 21st Century

Today's very successful companies such as Amazon, Netflix, and Ant Group are different from traditional companies. Amazon uses AI to recommend the products each customer is most likely to buy. Over 70% of the videos subscribers watch from Netflix come of recommendations based on previous choices. Ant Group uses AI to decide customers' requests for loans in seconds, delighting customers and at the same time being more productive. Ant Group employs fewer than 20,000 employees to serve a billion customers. By comparison, Bank of America employs 209,000 employees to serve 67 million customers with fewer products and services[1]. All three companies are enjoying unparalleled levels of success. To reach this winning point, companies must do much more than implement an AI application.

Leaders must follow three steps to upgrade a company to the 21ˢᵗ Century: enable the AI organization, have frictionless core processes and upgrade to a digital business model while implementing AI. Figure 3 shows these steps in the framework to move a business to the digital age. Companies do not need to be born-digital to be successful today. Still, they must adapt to the customers' new expectations with the help of new technologies.

Framework for Upgrading the Company to the 21st Century

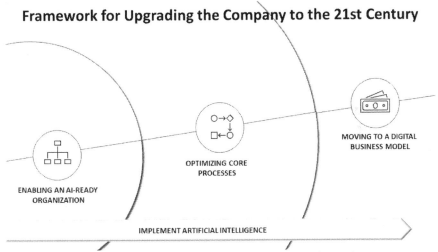

Figure 3. Framework for upgrading the company to the 21ˢᵗ Century

The first step in moving a business to the 21ˢᵗ Century is to enable an AI-ready organization. The actions in this step include learning about AI, setting the correct expectations, identify possible uses, and helping the organization be open for change. The second part is to optimize the core processes. AI's value is small if used in processes where one step is executed very fast only to advance to the following step where it must wait for a response from a human. AI in an optimized process can give customers instant services to customers. The last part is upgrading the business model to an omnichannel or digital ecosystem model where the company can leverage the network connections to provide comprehensive services to customers and sell more. Concurrent with these three steps, the organization must start to experiment and implement the first AI project.

Moving a business to the 21st Century has many rewards. Today, successful companies manage larger volumes and easily add products and services without further investments. These companies found that AI algorithms that run one type of transaction can easily be adapted to handle different transactions. An additional benefit is that as AI algorithms ingest large amounts of data, the company continues to learn and improve. Traditional companies are mainly static, with some minor improvements implemented by a few employees. The new AI-powered solutions learn 24 hours a day and find new ways to operate the business.

Two factors determine the value of a company, the business model and its core processes. A business model is the design of a business identifying revenue sources, customers, products, and financing. The company's processes enable the organization to serve its customers. The business model defines the theory, and the processes define the practice[1]. A 10-year study conducted by Harvard professors Marco Iansity and Karim Lakhani showed that the companies taking full advantage of AI operate with a new set of business models and processes, very differently from traditional companies.

Enabling an AI-ready organization

The first step in the framework for upgrading a business to the 21 Century is to prepare the organization for AI. Enabling an AI-ready organization is the first of the seven points most leaders do not know when implementing AI and is necessary to compete with this technology.

> **Point 1 – Enabling the organization to use AI**

An AI-ready organization is one whose members are familiar with AI concepts, can identify examples of AI uses, is data-driven, and are eager to embrace the change. Implementing the technology is the easy part. The hard part is to have an organization open and ready for change. The preparation must include all members of the organization. These are the steps needed to have an organization enabled for AI:

Learn about AI. The first step is for all levels of the organization to learn more about AI. This book accomplishes this task. Online courses are available on AI for executives. Make sure these courses offer practical ways to use AI today. Leaders should focus on AI strategic courses rather than technical ones. Spending one hour per day studying a particular subject for one year will make you more knowledgeable in that specific topic than 99% of the world's population.

Winning in today's AI age will ultimately depend on the workforce. The employees with the right skills will adopt AI as part of the team. Offer employees the opportunities to learn new skills to help them transition to the new roles working with AI. Define the job descriptions of the new positions and publish them when the hiring process starts. Notify internal employees of these new roles and offer them training to qualify for the jobs before hiring outside$_2$. Be sure to provide executives with training opportunities on AI's strategic uses, such as making better decisions and looking for new ways to use AI. Some positions, such as digital marketing experts and data scientists, may be filled from outside the company.

Set realistic expectations about AI. Some persons still perceive artificial intelligence as something fantastic and even superhuman. For many people, the first image that comes to mind is Terminator. As organizations prepare to develop their first AI projects, the leaders must work with all organizational levels to understand AI and have realistic expectations. Having employees with the wrong expectations is one of the fastest ways to fail with AI. Executives and senior business leaders should know what AI is and what AI can do for the company. Leaders working on AI projects should define the project direction, allocate resources, and monitor progress. Everyone in the organization should know that AI development is an iterative process, with multiple attempts to succeed. Consider including investor relations in the communication.

Identify AI examples in all industries. People learn through examples. Look up ways in which companies in your industry have applied AI. These are good ways to get an idea of how AI can be used in your business. The best ideas, however, will come from how companies outside your industry use AI. Adopting AI practices in your industry will give you advantages, but you will be a follower. Taking ideas from other industries and adapting them to your industry will make you a leader. Many creative uses of AI can identify by simply adapting the ideas of other industries and applying them to your own company.

Develop a thirst for data. The most critical step to prepare for implementing artificial intelligence is to convince all employees of the importance of data. Successful companies make increasing the use of data an essential element of their organizational culture. The most potent message leaders can send their organization is analyzing the data before making a decision. When leaders repeatedly base the significant decisions on data and analytics, employees start to see how analytics can provide new perspectives that even the brightest or more experienced executive could not know.

Firms must regard every project as an opportunity to obtain new data so AI can increase its knowledge. Most data is not clean, so organizations must apply tools to clean the data. Before considering doing an AI pilot project or buying an application, the organization needs to have data. The quality and scope of the data will determine the usefulness of the artificial intelligence applications.

AI feeds on data. Companies need massive amounts of clean data to use AI. Even after collecting and cleaning the data, businesses find it challenging to capture the value from data. The information by itself is not enough to leverage digital opportunities[3]. With AI, insights and decisions can happen faster with less human intervention. Business leaders now realize the correct use of technology is now changing the way companies compete. Successful companies have changed their self-perception to be technology first, retail (or their industry) second. Data is the new electricity, but data combined with human intuition can yield superior results.

Many leaders wrongly believe that they have all the data needed for AI when distributed on several servers and laptops. When these leaders try to start their AI initiative, they will discover that most of the work to prepare the data still needs to be done. The information needs to be identified, organized, placed in repositories, and cleaned. A recent survey indicates over 85% of corporations have started a data-driven culture initiative. Data is the heart of artificial intelligence. The machine learning part of AI will ingest the data to form new perspectives. If the information is incomplete or biased, AI solutions may provide incorrect insights.

Create a digital culture. An organization must accept artificial intelligence and other digital transformation changes to succeed in today's environment. Organizations that operate as they did during the 20ᵗʰ Century, especially those highly profitable, will be hesitant to embrace a digital culture. For these companies, there is not much hope. Eventually, competitors with a superior business model and digital technology to give customers personalized services will overtake them. Creating a digital culture means defining a vision of how digital technology could dramatically change the business. The cultural change must be from the top down. Top management must communicate multiple times to all employees how the digital vision will benefit the company and the employees and invite them to participate.

At Schneider Electric, the executive committee had periodic management meetings to review the business, the people, and the strategy. They decided to add a fourth review, the role of digital technology[4]. Schneider also added two new units, one for digital customer experience and another for digital services. The digital customer experience unit designs the digital customer journey. The digital services organization looks after the digital business transformation by helping the business areas manage their digital operation[4]. AI is a crucial part of the digital transformation and is usually applied with other technologies such as internet of things, biometrics, and cloud.

Help the organization embrace change. People naturally tend to resist all changes. The leaders must help their people to overcome resistance to the coming changes. As a first step, leaders must empower employees to adapt to the changes by providing the training they need, having experts available to consult if a problem arises, and recognizing when they accomplish the changes. The leaders themselves must set the example by welcoming and supporting the change. Any significant change implies mistakes. Wise leaders accept these mistakes without penalizing the employees. Once a manager admonishes an employee for making a mistake while attempting to implement a change, none of the other employees will dare propose or work on a change.

Set up a budget to experiment with AI. AI is still a new technology, and businesses must learn how it applies to them and how to use it. Include enough funds to bring AI experts such as data analysts, machine learning engineers, and business intelligence analysts in-house or outsourced. The entire initiative may cost between 20,000 and 300,000 to implement. Set up a budget with a fraction of these numbers initially. Most of the budget will need to be justified later on when the use cases are visible.

Leverage digital networks to increase traffic. Network effects are the value added by increasing the network's number of connections and with separate networks. A LinkedIn user has links with the business contacts who have accepted the invitation to join the network. That same LinkedIn user also receives invitations to apply to jobs compatible with the skillset in the profile. The more data gushes into a business, the more information the company has, the more AI can learn to improve the user experience or present targeted advertisers to the user.

21ˢᵗ Century companies know the value of digital networks and use them to improve business results. Imagine how much Facebook would be worth with only one user versus how much it is worth today with its almost 3 billion users. As companies connect with multiple networks, they gain access to other potential clients and new data flows that add to the network and learning effects[1].

An example of the use of network effects is an app for new parents. The app was initially planned for parents to record the baby's size, weight, and milestones during its first two years of life. In return, the parents would receive advice on how the baby is developing compared with other babies and answer the usual questions new parents commonly have. Once many parents used the app, other providers of related services found the network valuable. For example, pediatricians wanted to track the size and weight of the baby for possible deviations. Parents wanted the app to answer routine questions and alert them when a condition needed a trip to the hospital. Pharmacies wished to know the formula and medicines given to the baby to replenish an order before the parents' stock at home ran out. Insurers wanted to be kept in the loop to monitor the baby's health. Above all, the parents decided they wanted to be in the same network as other new parents to have ongoing conversations and exchange tips. What started as a simple app became a set of networks, each providing additional value to its users. Each network needs to be analyzed because each has unique properties and may interest different users[1].

Experiment, learn, and continue to improve using information. Companies today receive massive amounts of data from their networks, applications, points of sale, suppliers, social media, websites, and other channels. After cleaning and organizing this data, it becomes food for the AI applications. It also provides superb opportunities to run experiments to test a variety of operational and service issues.

Google and other major corporations do not rely on opinions to make decisions; they conduct experiments by formulating hypotheses. Google tests each idea in a randomized control trial, commonly known as an A/B test. In these experiments, a random sample of users works with the change, and the second group of users is the control group with no exposure to the change[1]. When the experiment ends, the experiment leader analyzes the outcomes to detect a statistically significant difference. Google uses data from its four billion users to run more than 400,000 experiments per year. A multifunctional team reviews the data from these experiments, and they approve the change. In 2019, Google ran over 400,000 experiments resulting in over 3,600 improvements[5]. Procter & Gamble also uses data to run experiments. P&G is now running 10,000 times more experiments than it did a decade ago. Amazon, Facebook, and Microsoft also conduct thousands of tests each year.

Experimentation is necessary to use AI well. Imagine that after running an algorithm to predict customer churn, the algorithms indicate that the customers most likely to stop buying are twenty-somethings. At this point, the company does not know if these customers would react positively to a discount to remain as customers. Rather than offering a costly discount to millions of customers in their twenties, the company could try to do an A/B test on a group of customers to determine what percentage of the customers would remain because of the specific offer. The company can save millions of dollars by testing the ideas before implementing them.

Two decades ago, employees who dared to do a pilot project to test new technologies and the project failed would be fired. Fortunately, today's successful companies have the opposite mentality. Business leaders today may be fired for not implementing some new technologies. The success of today's rising corporations is not only how they use data and applications but how they continue to learn and innovate. Corporations today have plenty of information from their systems, networks, social media, and other sources. Feeding this information to AI systems results in companies learning and improving continually. Over time, the gap between the companies that learn and those that do not (or learn at a slow pace) will be significant enough to make them unable to catch later.

Renewed focus on learning results in more innovation. As technology continues to evolve at exponential speed, continuous learning is critical for organizations. Learning fuels formal innovation and improvement programs to develop new products and services. Innovation is essential to remain competitive. In recent times, corporations have increased their focus on learning and innovation to grow the business with new opportunities as they arise and to neutralize threats before they become present[1].

Adopt a change management model. The primary cause of the failure of AI initiatives is organizational resistance to change. Resistance to change is not new, but leaders can manage it well using any excellent change management models available today. Do not expect employees to welcome with open arms the changes to their jobs that AI will bring.

Resistance to change was already present over 200 years ago. Up to the end of the 18ᵗʰ Century, weavers and cotton spinners worked from home producing textiles. The pay was good, and the workers enjoyed their free time. Then came the Industrial Revolution, replacing traditional workers with specialized equipment that could produce more fabric with fewer workers who needed less training. Instead of working from their homes, workers now had to go each day to work to a dark, filthy factory. The Luddite movement emerged, rebelling against this change In Nottingham, England. Some workers tried to bargain with the owners to receive a share of the factory profits, but the owners refused. Other workers demanded a new tax on the factories' cloth to help support the workers who had lost their jobs. Still, other workers pleaded to slow down textile factories' construction to allow workers to learn new trades. The mill owners refused all their demands.

In 1811, workers covered their faces with coal to disguise themselves and destroyed six framing machines in a factory. The group then marched to the factory owners' homes and burned them down. Similar attacks spread to other towns in England, destroying almost 200 machines per month. This group called themselves Luddites, after Ned Ludd, an apprentice beaten by his boss and later retaliated by destroying the machinery. The Luddites were jealous of the industrialists' new wealth and thought they acquired it at the workers' expense. The Luddite movement became more active and violent, even assassinating some of the factory owners. The British army sent 14,000 troops to stop the Luddites, hanging two dozen Luddites and shipping 51 to Australia[1].

The Luddite movement happened over two centuries ago, but many current technology implementations share the same Luddites' feelings and reactions. In the early 19th Century, the Luddites burned down equipment. Today's workers do not set fire to computers or delete software, but resistance to new working methods exists. Resistance may be manifested from a simple "I don't have time" to "the new technology does not work in *this* company." Inwardly, the employees are hoping the change will go away, so they do not have to learn new skills and, above all, they do not run the risk of losing their jobs. The Luddites' jealousy of factory owners' new wealth may be analogous to today's wealth gap between traditional and technology company owners.

When presenting the organization with an artificial intelligence project, do not expect everyone to smile with open arms and say, "Oh, I am so glad we have this change." Resisting change is built-in as part of human nature. Managing the resistance to change in organizations is now a critical skill. Emerging technologies are evolving at an exponential rate, changing the way we live, work, and learn. Companies today demand agile and sometimes virtual change management to keep up with crisis-driven changes.

Significant changes such as the ones AI brings will have a considerable impact on the organization and its employees. Expecting to introduce AI and have everybody applaud does not happen. The reaction will be the same as the Luddites except for a bit more civilized. Employees will resist. Use change management to manage this resistance. There are over 200 change management models in the market; any major initiative must include one of these models to succeed. Companies always have the choice to combine models to suit their needs. Change management models are valuable because they describe the best practices to open the organization to accept the new initiative. Change models should be part of any significant project or program. Leaders are free to select the best-suited model for the organization, but they must use at least one model.

Only 30% of major change initiatives in corporations succeed. The main reason for this failure is not managing change correctly. Change management models and methodologies can overcome the pervasive resistance to change. Today's most used change management models are the ADKAR change management model, Kotter's eight steps for change, Lewin's three-stage model, and Kübler-Ross five-stage change management model. Each change management model has different elements, but all share these essential components:

Change models may vary in their approach, but most have these elements in common:

- Define the change.
- Need for executive support.
- Communicate to all levels in the organization.
- Train people as needed.
- Develop the plans.
- Execute the plans.
- Adjust and reinforce actions.

Define the vision for the change. The first step in many change-management models is defining the change, what it is and what it is not. This step may sound trivial, but if the change is not defined clearly, each person will have a different version of the change, and the initiative will fail. A vision describes the future change for the organization, while a compelling vision creates a sense of urgency. The 2020 pandemic sparked the urgency for change. A good vision will communicate what the change implies and what it does not. Employees often panic thinking the change will bring significant upheavals in their area of responsibility when it will not. The vision statement must be easy to understand by everyone to end all speculation. Without a clear vision, leaders will need to spend additional time answering employees' questions and obtain less commitment[6].

A compelling vision must communicate the "why" of the change. The "why" connects the vision to specific actions employees can do and motivates them to work on the change. The best vision statements are short and easy to remember. Describe the current state, the future state, and why it needs to move to the future state.

Even project members who understand the changes AI will bring may not consistently articulate the initiative so the rest of the employees can understand and act on it. Leaders of a significant change initiative must work with the team members to develop a compelling vision.

Define the reason for the change. The reason must be compelling, so employees feel motivated to contribute. Validate the vision by asking employees what it means for them and what actions they would take. The leaders must focus the vision on the change. It is sad to see vision statements that promise everything one would want on this earth. The message conveyed by these types of words is that nobody understands the change, and management does not understand what a vision is. Avoid vision statements that leave readers unsure of the difference. The third step is to define a brief vision that is easy to remember. Avoid overused phrases such as "premier provider" or "best customer experience." The vision must inspire but be unique for your organization. The last step should be to describe the before and after states. A clear vision describes the current and the new situations to have a clear concept of the change.

Develop a change management plan. The change management plan is different from the project plan. The change management plan manages the change process, budget, resources, scope, schedule, and communication under control. The change management plan will minimize the impact a change can have on the stakeholders and the project. The program should contain specific tasks, the person responsible, and the target date. Define all the steps to be done to reach the vision, including communication and training. Employees must know what the change is about, what it will do, and what it will not do before they feel comfortable and give their cooperation.

Employees will need new skills to adapt to their work changes and have AI become part of the team. Some employees who will not be using AI may show interest in receiving AI training as it is regarded as a novelty. Focus training on those persons who will need the new skills. The rest of the employees may be given a general orientation about AI or point out resources available on the web, such as Coursera's AI courses. Along with the training, appoint subject matter experts in the areas using AI. Having a trusted peer available to answer questions or clear up doubts will help employees make the transition.

Use complaints positively. Some leaders think employees who complain about the change are ill-intentioned and want to destroy the change initiative. Leaders who feel this way are committing a severe error and are letting go of a golden opportunity to advance AI acceptance in the organization. Employees who voice concern are showing they care enough about the initiative to take the trouble to complain. When an employee expresses a complaint, leaders should listen and, if necessary, act. Ignoring or dismissing the complaint may harm the initiative because the complaint may be valid, and other employees may feel the same way, only they are not voicing the problem.

Complaints are helpful because they help leaders understand the issues behind the complaint. Leaders need to address the complaint issues and communicate to the employee the actions taken to solve them. Confirming that the employee has no other complaints is a good idea.

Use transformational leadership. Transformational leadership occurs when a leader and employees interact in ways that raise performance and motivation. Transformational leadership has four dimensions: idealized influence, inspirational motivation, intellectual stimulation, and empowerment. Idealized influence is the leader's ability to earn respect and admiration for his followers so that they want to imitate their leaders. The transformational leader must work to increase the optimism, enthusiasm, and attention of the followers. Intellectual stimulation. The transformational leader of elevating employees to make them more aware, innovative, and creative. Delegate employees to respond directly to customer requests and problems[7].

When implementing AI, organizational resistance to change is not the only problem to be encountered. AI fundamentally changes how we do many of our daily activities, and several ethical challenges have already become evident. Leaders in organizations must be aware of these dilemmas as AI is implemented and manage them to prevent potential problems.

Leverage peer advocates. A powerful way to convince the employees of the need to change is to leverage peer advocates. Peer advocates are employees from any level in the organization that understand and support the change. The initiative leaders need to identify the peer advocates in their organization, provide them with training and ask them to disseminate the need for change.

Employees are more likely to believe the change is necessary if they hear it from their peers than from someone at the top. Employees will feel more comfortable asking peers for advice on applying the new practices when confronted with problems. Empowering peer advocates to convince and help others with the change will multiply the organization's efforts.

Sometimes peer advocates take the form of self-organizing teams that can be very valuable in implementing the change. An example happened during the pandemic when IBM employees transitioned from working in the office to working from home. A group of employees took the responsibility to establish guiding principles to make remote work more manageable. This group worked with HR leaders to expand their efforts to the rest of the company. Within days, thousands of employees had publicly committed via internal social media to using the new principles. The CEO shared his commitment on LinkedIn. The grassroots effort accelerated the adoption of productive remote work faster than any formal corporate initiative could have[6].

Identify the level of commitment to the change. In every change, people will join one of these four groups: (a) a minority of early adopters of the change, (b) those willing to adopt the change but would prefer to wait to see what the early adopters do, this group is more numerous than the previous group, (c) people who like to wait until others have widely implemented the change, the majority falls in this category, and (d) a small group of persons will refuse to adapt to the change. For the latter group, it is better to work with Human Resources. If they still refuse to change, there may be no hope for them.

The persons in groups 1 and 2 are valuable because they can play a role as peer advocates. Some persons accept the change after they witness peers convinced of the change and already practicing it. If these peers have already incorporated the initiative in their daily job, the rest will perceive there is life after the change, and it is all right to accept it. Some change leaders focus on group 4, trying to convince them to welcome the change. Doing so is a mistake because this group may not accept the initiative. Leveraging the enthusiasm of groups 1 and 2 will yield more results than wasting time with group$_4$.

Resistance to change among employees is inevitable. Instead of blaming employees for not embracing the change, influential leaders work with them, accepting their complaints and rumors and addressing their concerns. Addressing rumors in the open prevents them from growing and damaging the organizational climate.

Optimizing core processes

Successful companies optimize core processes before implementing AI. When all the steps in a process are automated, and the bottlenecks are removed, the customer can receive immediate service. Optimizing core processes is the second of the seven points leaders must use to leverage AI.

> **Point 2 – Eliminating core processes bottlenecks**

If human intervention is needed, customers must wait for hours or days before receiving an answer. When customers receive a prompt response from one company, they naturally expect the same response from other companies. When they do not receive the same level of service, the customers will buy more from companies giving them better service.

Typically, half of the steps in business processes do not add value to the company or the customers. Process improvement or Lean are techniques for identifying and removing non-value-added steps. By removing the "waste" in the steps of a process, the errors and time to execute are reduced. Having a smooth process is necessary so AI can provide prompt responses to customers. Automating a process without eliminating unnecessary steps will be more costly and time-consuming and ultimately lead to executing unnecessary steps faster.

Digital financial services are already receiving requests for loans, processing them, and either awarding the loan or rejecting it without intervention from humans. Operating in a digital frictionless environment means having a smooth operation and multiplying the number of customers at an unprecedented rate. Facebook delivers news and information services to more persons than those served by the entire US postal system[1]. Operating without bottlenecks requires more than just implementing an AI application. It requires redesigning the process end-to-end from the start point to the endpoint.

Newly designed processes only consist of the steps needed to do a task. As time goes by, new regulations, new managers with bright ideas, and new compliance rules add steps required at the time but are never removed when they are no longer needed. As technology evolves, parts of the process are automated, but nobody pays attention to the delays in the process. These delays are part of the waste most processes have. These are the leading eight types of waste in processes:

1. Overproduction such as extra copies, unnecessary emails from a chain of "reply to all," or unused information.
2. Unnecessary waiting, such as approval from a supervisor or waiting for material.
3. Unnecessary transportation such as transferring a call to another department in a call center or moving equipment.
4. Overprocessing. Unnecessary approvals for a proposal.
5. Unnecessary inventory such as extra supplies or unused tools and files.
6. Unnecessary movement such as extra clicks to accomplish a task or double entry of data.
7. Excessive defects such as errors or scrapping a product.
8. Underused resources such as talents not used or idle assets.

Fortunately, organizations can remove these forms of waste in processes. If a process is extensive, improving the process will be a project effort. In all cases, these are the steps to remove waste:

1. Identify the process to be improved, define the start and end points, and obtain the commitment from a sponsor. Select a team leader and a multifunctional team. The multifunctional team must consist of at least one person from each area involved in executing the process. Define the critical business problem to be solved; just vaguely trying to improve a process will not work. Define a date for the team to meet to work on the process. Gather preliminary data to define the baseline.
2. Meet with the team. Present to the team the eight types of waste. Review the problem, scope, and data. Map the current process.
3. The team identifies the waste in the process and discusses how to eliminate them.
4. The team maps the future process after brainstorming possible solutions and approaches.
5. Develop an action plan with the changes to implement the new processes. Assign owners to each action plan.
6. Define the steps to prevent backsliding to the previous process. Implement training, new metrics, and a recognition system for employees successfully using the new process.

Eliminating human and organizational bottlenecks from the customer's critical path significantly impacts the operation of a company[1]. Once the teams remove the blockages in the process, and implement AI, the marginal cost of serving additional customers is close to zero. Less redundant steps require less staff and bureaucracy[1]. The remaining employees involved with the process no longer deliver the product or service. The supervisor will oversee the software-automated AI algorithm that does the work.

Process improvement enables AI to flow through core processes without bottlenecks resulting in a superior experience for the customer. AI improves the processes by solving problems. Changes in processes are necessary as AI takes over specific tasks and employees´ transition to new tasks.

The traditional processes limit enterprises as they try to grow—the bigger the company, the more complexity, and problems it faces. For example, hiring many new employees simultaneously to keep up with demand means some new hires will need time to ramp up, make the typical rookie mistakes, and some may not adapt to the organization and end up leaving. Launching many new products within a short time may harm a company as operational cost increases while service levels go down. AI solutions and digital networks enable companies to (a) achieve economies of scale, (b) offer a wider diversity of products and services, and (c) continue to learn to keep improving. Optimizing core processes provides two strategic advantages to businesses: sell more to customers and sell additional types of products without adding resources.

Sell to more customers without adding resources. Selling to more customers without additional resources is scaling a business. Scaling a business means adding revenue at a fast rate while increasing cost at a low rate. An example of scale is serving more customers in a fast-food restaurant while only increasing cost minimally. When Microsoft develops new software, it has initial development and marketing expenses, but it can sell the software to as many people as possible without further increasing its costs.

Organizations can grow in a scalable way by applying analytics and AI to their operations. A new kind of enterprise that uses digital components is surpassing traditional companies and even changing the economy. The new type of business is operating with software, analytics, and AI instead of human-centric processes. The result is these new businesses can grow in a frictionless way and are more scalable. Companies such as Amazon, Microsoft, and Airbnb can expand quickly because their processes are clean, automated, and use AI. Companies that increase their digitization levels, analytics, and AI use can vastly improve the business's scalability, providing more value as the number of customers increases. The automated processes and the extensive amounts of data they handle with analytics allow them to move into other industries, such as Alibaba setting up a bank.

Sell additional types of products without adding resources. When traditional businesses grow, either by selling more of the same product or selling other types of products, they need to hire and train additional employees and make investments to handle the extra workload. Anyone can relate to long lines to pay for an item at a mall on the Saturday before Christmas or the confusion at a busy bank branch with new employees who need to call the supervisor for every transaction, or the panic buying when the pandemic broke out.

Over the last ten years, some companies have begun to operate differently. These companies are using optimized processes with artificial intelligence systems capable of executing end-to-end processes without human intervention. As a result, when these companies sell more products or add a new type of product, they can grow with the same resources enabled by digital technologies. When Amazon adds new products, customers continue to access the same friendly website, have the same convenient payment method, the new products are stored in the same warehouse and carried by the same robots to the same shipping point. The cost of Amazon when it adds new products is negligible due to the way it operates with artificial intelligence, machine learning, and robotics[1]. Contrast Amazon to a brick-and-mortar store that adds new products. The retail company would probably need to hire additional buyers and store personnel to handle the extra workload. The company buyers would need to define the new goods to carry in stores and contact and evaluate the suppliers. Store operations would need to assign shelf space and decide which products to eliminate or reduce their presence on the shelves to make room for the products. Marketing would need to run pricing scenarios to determine the correct price and introductory discounts. In a physical retail store, adding a new line of products would mean hiring additional salespersons. Someone able to selling electronics may not do so well when trying to sell children's clothes. In contrast, Amazon can add new product lines without adding complexity or hiring more staff.

Companies can now provide new services. Advanced analytics and AI are now enabling companies to learn more about each customer. For example, cameras, sensors, computer vision, and deep learning algorithms give Walmart a close look at how customers shop in a store and can replicate the online shopping experience as if the customer were physically in the store[1]. By analyzing data of the items purchased by customers, retail companies can now remind customers if they forget an item. Some retailers analyze the goods purchased to infer if the customer had a significant life event, such as starting to work for the first time or if a baby is on the way to determine the new items the customer will be needing. These recommendations to online shoppers increase sales and provide customers with suggestions of items they may need.

Reduce silos. Eliminating unnecessary steps translates into silo reduction. As companies grew during the 19th Century, the managers realized they needed to structure the organization in a hierarchy to have accountability and manageable pieces[8]. Over the last 200 years, many companies operated in siloed structures. These companies build processes around the silos, and later the applications follow the silos. Due to siloed operations, companies had low visibility into order fulfillment operations, causing revenue loss, overpayments, and compliance issues. Silos are an obstacle to achieving frictionless digitized processes. Optimized core processes permit businesses to reach new levels of scalability with a broader scope and innovation, in essence, transforming the critical path to deliver value[1].

Upgrading to a digital business model

Artificial intelligence is giving companies the capability to compete in new ways. Some companies have moved to new business models using the new flexibilities AI provides, achieving new profitability levels.

Digital transformation is not about technology; it is about business change. A digital company is an organization that uses technology in its internal and external operations as a competitive advantage[9]. Digital companies have business models that enable changes in their activities, including adding new income sources as new technologies emerge[9]. Companies in a traditional business model can improve profitability by moving first to an omnichannel model and later to the ecosystem model. The ecosystem business model offers the highest profitability. Without a compelling vision to succeed in the digital economy, companies may die a painful death[4].

A business model is simply a description of how a business makes money. A business model is the combination of resources that create value for the company and the clients through exchanges. Resources alone do not bring value to the company; the value comes from exchanging resources[10]. Technology can create value if it is used or exchanged in a digital business model. The phrase "business model" was first used in 1957 by Richard Bellman to refer to a business simulation in the real world through a model. Faster and cheaper computing power gives rise to the prevalent use of sensors, networks, artificial intelligence, 3D printing, robotics, and blockchain, among others. The convergence of these technologies is resulting in new business models[11]. With the advent of information and communication technology in the late 20th Century, the term business model was used to mean how an internet-based company (.com) became a traditional company. Today, the business model is used by all types of companies, including Al-Qaida[10].

Business models have seven functions:

1. Show how to create value for customers.
2. Recognize the market and its mechanism to generate income.

3. Define the structure of the value chain.
4. Clarify the source of the income.
5. Predict the cost structure and potential profit.
6. Describe the company's role in the network to create value that connects customers, including identifying complementary companies.
7. Formulate a competitive strategy to gain an advantage over competitors.

Many confuse the terms "business model" and "strategy." A strategy is the plan to achieve the vision, including the choice of business model. All organizations have a business model, but they do not necessarily have a strategy[10]. A digital business model has three parts:

1. Digital Value Proposition - includes products and services, customers, and strategy.
2. Network architecture - includes connections to vendors, partners, customers, organization, and resources and capabilities.
3. Capturing digital value - formulation of how to build and sustain capabilities and competencies over competitors, as well as financial and non-financial assets[12].

Some leaders still believe that setting up a digital business is merely launching an app or a website. Isolated actions such as these are rarely successful. The digital business should be based, among other things, on a sound digital business model. Hundreds of companies have undergone a digital transformation. These companies have created new value propositions, often with innovative ways to deliver a superior customer experience through technology[4]. 21st-century companies create value by giving customers something new and important and creating experiences that customers want to repeat.

Throughout history, industries have organized themselves as linear value chains: they bought raw materials, made products, and sold them. As digital technologies advance, digital ecosystems are emerging as a more profitable business model using today's technologies[13]. Companies in the 1980s followed Michael Porter's competitive advantage model. These companies purchased raw materials, processed these materials into products, and sold the products. To gain a competitive advantage was to either sell at a lower cost than competitors or offer a different and superior product. These companies had well-defined and controlled value chains. At that time, organizations did not know much about the customer's needs and life events. Today's market is different. Corporations now compete with complex, networked competitors who understand the customers and are engaging with them. There are several digital business models in today's world. Each organization uses one of these business models predominantly, but most will operate in more than one of these models[4]. These are the three main models as shown in figure 4; each has unique characteristics and financial results:

Digital Business Models

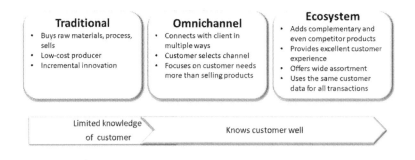

Figure 4. Digital business models

Moving up to a digital business model is the third of the seven points leaders frequently miss in implementing AI.

> **Point 3 – Upgrading to an omnichannel or ecosystem business model**

Traditional business model. The traditional business model works in a value chain with suppliers. It worked well in the marketplace of the late 20th Century, but today it is falling behind. Companies with this business model have little knowledge of their customers; they sell through other companies. Typically, suppliers are enterprises that sell insurance via independent agents (Metlife), electronic devices such as TVs via retailers (Samsung), or mutual funds via brokers (Vanguard)[4]. Suppliers are losing power and must reduce prices even as they continue digitizing. Procter & Gamble counterbalanced with a campaign to learn more and connect to its more than four billion consumers using branding, social media, and direct-to-customer approaches[4].

Omnichannel business model. Firms with an omnichannel model provide customers access to their products and services across many digital and physical channels. In this business model, businesses know their clients very well and accompany them in every event in their lives[4]. An early form of omnichannel marketing happened in the 1890s when Sears, Roebuck, and Company issued catalogs with pictures and descriptions of products customers could buy. New online sales channels appeared a century later with the arrival of the internet[14]. The first electronic transaction was an album sold between two persons in August 1994. A few days later, Pizza Hut became the first company to sell a product via the internet[14]. Prompt digital delivery of services makes customers happy and more inclined to buy from you again.

Examples of companies that use an omnichannel business model are Nordstrom, Carrefour, Origin Energy, Walmart, Citibank, and Canadian Imperial Bank of Commerce, CIBC, among others[4]. USAA, a bank that serves only the US military, is focused on providing its clients a superior customer experience. When USAA detects a customer is going through a life event such as buying a car, getting married, moving, or having a child, USAA is prepared to offer an integrated package to handle all the financial needs for that event.

For example, if a person purchases a car, USAA offers a car loan, extended vehicle warranty, car insurance, maintenance guide, and the previous vehicle's sale[4].

Companies using the omnichannel business model track the products viewed by customers regardless of the device. Retailers detect when a customer views the same article several times but does not buy, meaning there is an obstacle. Instead of just reminding the customer to purchase the item, the retailer sends an email with a discount[4]. Should the customer still resist buying, the company will place ads on the internet sites the customer visits. If the customer does not buy after a few weeks of placing online ads, the company may change tactics. If the customer was looking at a computer printer, the company might send ads for recycled ink cartridges[4]. Persistent companies may go a step further and mail a paper ad so the customer can see the printing quality.

Businesses operating with an omnichannel focus on the customers' needs, not just on selling products. These businesses have efficient operations because they do not have to gather information with each interaction. The customers feel valued because of the personalized experience and are likely to be more loyal. However, the omnichannel business model requires heavy technology investment to integrate all channels[4].

Ecosystem business model. Ecosystems are a network of coordinated companies, devices, and clients that create value for all participants. Ecosystems give customers a shopping experience with a wide array of products and services from complementary suppliers and sometimes even competitors without a hierarchical authority[4]. Ecosystems have the best performance in net margin, revenue growth, customer experience, and innovation and are the goal for many companies[4]. Ecosystems help companies to be successful by adding complementary products and making them available digitally[4]. Thriving ecosystems require a platform, a network of participants, products or services, and the market's expectation to satisfy users' needs[4]. COVID-19 proved companies' need to be either in the omnichannel or the ecosystem business models to thrive. Many of the companies in the traditional model suffered painful losses. The significant risk for a company that is not part of an ecosystem or that does not have an ecosystem strategy is that it is left behind, loses the market, and may even go bankrupt[13].

The most famous example of a company operating with an ecosystem business model is Amazon. Amazon offers customers a wider assortment of products than any store, usually at the best price, with the luxury of the customer reading other buyers' comments about the products (something that is not available at a physical store) and making the payments process simple. Amazon has third-party vendors that sell similar and sometimes identical products. Amazon and the customer provide timely feedback to the vendors to improve. Amazon uses artificial intelligence to learn about the customers' preferences from the searches done by each customer and the item purchased. Other companies that also use an ecosystem business model are:

Aetna. Aetna in 2000 was a B2B health insurance operating in a traditional business model. By 2010, Aetna decided to learn more about their customers to provide them with superior service and moved to an omnichannel business model. Aetna first implemented an easy, Amazon-style way of paying for insurance. The next step was to gather information about their clients from several sources to integrate a 360-degree view of each customer. Since many customers were on social media, Aetna installed sentiment analysis software to determine whether Aetna's conversations were positive or negative. Aetna applied analytics to their new information to identify and provide customers with more value. Lastly, they acquired several apps to improve health and physical condition and made them available to their clients[4].

Five years later, Aetna decided to move to the ecosystem business model. Their goal was to become a place where the customer could find the help they needed for their health and wellness needs. Aetna purchased apps to navigate symptoms and alert customers when they should go to the emergency room. Aetna also partnered with other companies to provide content, data, and additional services to Aetna's customers[4]. At this point, Aetna installed artificial intelligence applications to handle claims so the staff could have more time to focus on clients.

Schneider Electric. Schneider Electric, founded in 1836, was a traditional steel and manufacturing company making initially heavy machinery and later elevators and maintaining them. Electric Schneider's business doubled between 2002 and 2008, but the growth created complexity, inefficiencies, and loss of revenue opportunities; customers and employees complained. Even smaller companies could offer products like Schneider's at a lower cost. In 2009, Schneider changed its business model from a manufacturer of electrical products (traditional model) to a provider of intelligent energy automation solutions (an ecosystem driver). Schneider decided it wanted to be a destination for its customers, selling Schneider's products and other products in interconnected systems. Instead of limiting themselves to manufacturing and maintaining elevators, Schneider decided to be a "provider of intelligent energy management and automation solutions"[4]. Schneider placed sensors in their equipment to alert them when a specific part was wearing down. Instead of waiting until an elevator broke down, usually full of people, Schneider could service the piece ahead of time, become a service provider in addition to a manufacturer. Today's elevator sensors send more than 200 million messages per day to communicate their state, reduce waiting time for passengers, and alert them of potential problems[4].

To determine its digital business model, the leaders must decide if they belong to a value chain controlled by a key player (traditional model) or part of a digital ecosystem where the dynamics are about using networks (ecosystem)[4]. A higher level of knowledge of their customers points to omnichannel or ecosystem business models. With this information, firms can determine which business model they are using now.

The next step is to select which business model they want to be. Businesses should consider moving to an ecosystem. The ecosystem business model outperforms other models in customer experience, time to market, revenue growth, and net profit margin[4]. The other reason to move to an ecosystem is the pressure from customers who have used several ecosystems and want a similar experience[4]. Most existing business today develop their customer relationships even more and take advantage of their networks.

For a company in a value chain to move to a digital ecosystem, a first step is to move to an omnichannel by learning more about their customers and seamlessly offering multiple channels. The next is to open the company to more alliances and learn more about its client. Most of the companies use the traditional model. Companies must move to omnichannel and then the ecosystem model. Moving from the traditional model directly to the ecosystem model will not work as it will require excessive rework. Recent surveys show that large corporations tend to use traditional and omnichannel business models. It is common to find start-ups using the ecosystem business model. These companies, which started operations during the 21ˢᵗ Century, were born organized to profit from today's technology; they were born digital[4].

A transition from value chains to ecosystems is already happening; an example is Apple that works together with developers, suppliers, customers, etc. Perhaps not all companies can develop their ecosystem. Still, leaders must know how to participate in an ecosystem since it is a way to organize themselves to create value[13]. The increase in companies that become ecosystems will lead to a consolidation in several industries. The number of thriving ecosystems in a customer domain can only be a few[4].

Implementing AI

Implementing AI requires several steps, and organizations must start preparing early. Implementing AI crosses through each of the three phases of the framework for upgrading a company to the 21st Century. While the organization is learning about AI, leaders must motivate employees to develop a thirst for data. Collecting, cleaning, and organizing data should be done at the start of the AI initiative. The main reason AI initiatives suffer delays is the lack of sufficient data. During the second phase of the framework, the company should start experimenting and setting up a pilot project aligned with the core areas of the business. At this time, the organization should have acquired new data, skills, and technologies. Reviewing an existing process, eliminating non-value-added steps, and designing a new process will give teams a clear insight into which steps to use technological tools, including AI. By the time the organization is in the third phase, the organization should be scaling the pilot projects to production.

Concluding the chapter, the AI age brings many changes. Customers now demand an Amazon-like service for all purchases. New skills such as data science and analytics have surged worldwide to enable organizations to harness massive data worldwide. Social media and platform-based companies are giving corporations access to more extensive networks. Successful digital corporations operate very differently from the traditional ways of doing business. Digital organizations run based on data, with automated processes with no bottlenecks. They can achieve economies of scale, widen their scope with new products and services at no or little additional cost. A significant difference is that 21st Century companies keep learning and improving from the data they acquire. These companies use omnichannel or ecosystem business models resulting in higher profitability.

The following chapter describes how artificial intelligence is used in all industries and corporate disciplines to improve the customer experience, have a more competitive digital commerce, increase sales, reduce risk, improve productivity, and improve employee engagement. Through AI, leaders can approach marketing in new ways, retail can be more effective and profitable, but above all, AI is a crucial driver for digital transformation.

65 PROFITABLE WAYS TO USE AI

AI recognizes emotions, and that changes the customer experience. AI is not just about cost reduction but new ways of doing business and interacting with customers. AI could achieve more technological breakthroughs in the next 20 years than in humanity's entire history[1]. AI is transforming business with new insights and capabilities we did not have before. AI is changing the nature of work. As AI evolves, companies will find new ways to benefit from AI.

AI can alter the cost of many business activities and our daily lives, causing a ripple effect even higher than imagined. Using semiconductors as an analogy, every two years, their capacity doubles, and the price drops by 50%. In essence, semiconductors reduced the cost of arithmetic, and this happened:

1. We started using arithmetic more frequently. People stopped doing calculations such as demand planning manually and began using tools equipped with semiconductors simply because the tools were available at a reasonable cost.
2. Since arithmetic was less expensive and we had low-cost calculators and computers, we started to use the new cheaper arithmetic to solve problems not regarded as arithmetic problems. For example, people applied arithmetic to chemistry-based photography and later applied arithmetic to design and image reproduction for digital cameras.
3. As arithmetic costs continued to drop, other elements started to have a change in their value. For example, the value of arithmetic's complements, such as the hardware and software used in digital cameras, went up. On the other hand, the value of substitutes such as older film-based cameras' components went down because there was little or no demand for them[2].

The most common uses of AI today are in customer service, recommending other products, and fraud detection. AI is driving all industries to compete in new ways that were not possible previously. Ultimately, AI drives company growth.

The fourth point leaders need to know is learning the AI success in their industry. This chapter contains 65 examples, some apply to most industries while others are specific to a particular industry.

> **Point 4 – Learning about AI successes in your industry**

Learning how competitors and other industries use AI can be a source of innovation. AI dates from the 1950s but only recently have corporations started to use it. Since AI is a system that learns instead of having detailed instructions, the potential uses are all new. Taking the time to study how other industries are using AI is valuable to determine new applications. If business leaders limit their research to only looking within their industry, they will miss many opportunities. Applying what their own industry is doing will make them followers. Real innovation will come from looking at what other industries are doing and applying the concept, not the details, to their industry. These are some examples of how innovation came from ideas in other industries: (a) the umbrella baby stroller was inspired by the landing wheels of an airplane, (b) the concept of the McDonald's drive-thru came from the Formula 1 pit stops, (c) aerodynamic trains were designed following the shape of birds, (d) the idea of BMW's iDrive came from videogames joysticks and (e) the carton used to protect eggs now protects wines.

Applying ideas from other industries on how to use AI is point 5 of the seven points leaders must keep in mind:

> **Point 5 – Applying AI successful uses from other industries to your business**

This chapter describes 65 ways of using AI in lucrative ways by providing a better customer experience, improving digital commerce, increasing sales, reducing cost, enhancing productivity, reducing risk, and increasing employee engagement, among others, as shown in figure 5. Many of these examples incorporate AI with other technologies such as the internet of things and analytics.

Top Artificial Intelligence Cases

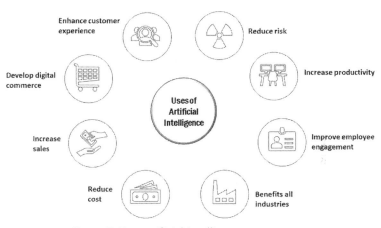

Figure 5. Top artificial intelligence use cases

Improve customer experience

Customer experience is a competitive growth driver when successful and the most significant risk when it fails[3]. Customer experiences rely on customer data insights, but these datasets can be messy and difficult to interpret. This complexity is the reason why AI is contributing much value to the customer experience. Salespeople, call center agents, and customer-facing employees know the customer's past purchases, experiences, and habits and act accordingly[3]. However, delivering a consistent experience across all channels requires knowing the customers' shopping patterns across a massive dataset. The only tool that provides this capability is artificial intelligence.

Artificial intelligence is now an essential tool for providing an exceptional customer experience. Combining AI, machine learning, massive data, and computing power enables brands to understand each customer personally. Traditional analytical tools worked with data and gave a result based on the specific data, but AI continuously learns from the data and can anticipate customer behavior[4]. Furthermore, the exponential data growth permits B2B and B2C brands to use AI to improve customers' everyday experiences.

AI can provide a personalized customer experience at all points of the customer journey. The results are new customer experiences and a journey that feels more natural to customers[3]. These are some ways AI improves the customer experience:

1. **Customer service 24/7**. Businesses can interact with customers 24/7 using AI-powered chatbots. Companies are willing to pay for personalized customer service using AIs[5]. AI can simultaneously interact with many customers and answer questions based on their past sales and browsing history. According to a recent survey, the leading reason for large companies to adopt AI is delivering a better customer experience[6].

2. **Identify customer needs through data**. AI can analyze massive amounts of data to learn each customer's preferences and needs. Amazon, for example, gives recommendations on an individual basis, even if two persons are looking at the same item. McDonald's drive-through menus now display meals that anticipate what customers want based on an AI application that uses the time of day, weather, and restaurant traffic data. Another example is the use of voice-to-text and text analyzers to convert the call center conversations to text and analyze the contents of those conversations, an opportunity not possible without AI.

3. **Serve customers in new ways**. Using AI-powered conversational chatbots, virtual agents can answer customer questions and even analyze why customers call repetitive times. The cases where customers call multiple times can be simplified to free human agents to answer complex inquiries.

AIs in banking can nudge the customer when the balance is getting low or send alerts when a significant payment is coming up[7].

Upgrade digital commerce

Digital commerce has a pre-COVID-19 era and a post-COVID-19 era. Retail digital trade grew by 27% in 2020, while overall physical store sales declined by 3%. Some online stores experienced 3x to 5x growth in revenue, with much higher margins. Customers who previously were distrustful or even afraid to buy via the internet now prefer online shopping over going to a store. AI plays a crucial role in the effectiveness of digital commerce. Here are some examples:

4. **Predicting trends**. AI can predict shopping trends, optimize warehouses, set prices, and personalize promotions for each customer. Knowing that a customer always buys six avocados per week enables the grocer to offer a customized list to ensure the customer does not forget the avocados. The retailer may even include in the list other items that go well with avocados[8].

5. **Providing an intuitive shopping experience**. Online stores with AI tools are giving customers an intuitive shopping experience. With cameras, image recognition, and machine learning, some retailers have already learned the typical path customers follow inside a store and replicate the same path in the online shopping experience.

6. **Personal shopping assistant**. Conversational-AI armed with a personalized knowledge of each customer, called conversational commerce, provides personal shopping assistance 24/7 in a friendly environment. Virtual assistants can engage with customers in casual conversation without being pushy "sales things." Innovative customizations make users feel they are understood, and the suggestions were made just for them[8]. AI-powered personal assistants are used mainly with customers but may also be used in internal

business systems to make them more friendly to users.

7. **Better inventory management**. AI-powered predictive analytics enables better inventory control based on historical data, predicts changes in product demands, and identifies potential logistics or weather issues that could affect inventory levels[8]. By knowing consumers' preferences and shopping patterns, retailers can forecast the inventory levels required with increased accuracy. AI-powered analytics can predict future behaviors with high accuracy.

8. **Search for better deals**. Virtual personal assistants such as Alexa and Siri will, in the future, be able to not only answer questions but search for better deals for their users. Imagine Alexa telling you it analyzed cell phone carriers in your area and found another telephone service provider that could reduce the annual bill by over $100 and, if you approve, it could make the switch with only your voice approval. If the other carrier is reputable, Alexa's proposal would not require much thinking. Users would save much if the Alexas of the world made similar proposals according to the carriers available in each country. Virtual assistants doing a similar analysis for other expenses such as gas utility, TV programming, insurance, and labs, among others, would increase savings. Consumers would benefit by saving without any effort.

Massive search for better deals may have some drawbacks. Once this practice, called hyperswitching, becomes widespread, AI could bring a new type of disruption to the market to the point of collapsing some firms[9]. When virtual personal assistants can search and analyze suppliers to offer their users the possibility of switching their services to other providers, major corporations face an upheaval. For example, if Alexa would advise its users to switch mobile phone carriers to its 100 million worldwide users and half of them accept Alexa's suggestion, significant market changes would occur.

Telecommunications companies such as AT&T and T-Mobile would see the consequential loss of clients.

In contrast, the companies favored by Alexa would see an almost instant boost in their businesses and possibly the physical inability to service many of its additional customers. This situation, hyperswitching, has several market and legal implications. Some banks, insurance companies, and even consumer companies have already started to prepare internally and externally for the possibility of hyperswitching. Internally, their systems must be ready to receive and answer the queries of 100 million Alexas asking for price and specifications. Externally, these companies have formed conglomerates to diversify revenues, increased cash holdings to buffer fluctuations in the market, and colluding with other companies on price to escape AIs scrutiny and enter volatility. Virtual assistants' massive queries are potentially drastic enough to warrant regulators to design laws to limit digital intermediaries[9]. Even if hyperswitching never arrives, the fears of large corporations could change capital markets and the economy. Memories of the Great Depression, when panic led bank customers to withdraw all their funds triggering economic upheaval, provides us lessons of what may occur. If AIs worldwide start comparing savings accounts interest rates among banks, find better alternatives, and their users approve the changes, banks could face a similar hardship. Only this time, machines would be withdrawing the money instead of people crowding bank branches. Widespread hyperswitching could cause business failures and unemployment. Experts and regulators' task is to improve risk monitoring and analyze possible scenarios[9].

Increase sales

Many companies have plenty of data in their corporate systems but do not know how to analyze it well enough to drive sales. The data used as learning material for AI can create predictive models about customers' behavior, market trends, and sales opportunities not yet detected. Data from corporate systems is generally cleaner data and is already available[10]. These are some of the possibilities for increasing sales:

9. **More accurate lead scoring**. For B2B sales, AI can analyze data such as corporate background, demographics, and financial situations, compare it with profiles stored and identify the prospect's characteristics that would make a sale likely. Analytics can also predict when to close a deal by correlating customer need with the product or service being sold[10].

10. **Guiding sales prospects**. AI with machine learning can automate personalized steps to nurture the sales process, handle objections and advance the prospect to where the sales rep is ready to close the sale. Analytics can improve sales offers based on each company's situation and analyze sales pitches showing which topics and subject lines work best[10].

11. **Reducing churn and upselling**. The cost of retaining a customer is a fraction of the cost to acquire new customers. Predictive analytics can give insights into customer satisfaction by alerting when a customer is not using the service enough, has problems with support, or needs new features. The predictive capacity can also identify when customers buy more by analyzing their product activity[10].

12. **Increasing Salespersons productivity**. Generating and managing contracts with customers is a time-consuming task for B2B salespersons. AI-enabled software is enabling users to manage contracts from creation to signature. In addition, the software automates reporting, tracking, and send reminders. As a result, sales teams can generate specialized contracts and deliver them to clients very quickly.

13. **Improving sales management**. AI and predictive analytics can help sales managers have more accurate sales quotas, optimize sales territories, realign sales compensation, make changes in staffing, and identify the potential impact of product changes on sales[10].

14. **Retaining customers through increased product usage**. Netflix feeds each customer's behavior and preferences data to AI to recommend other videos the viewer may find interesting. Netflix estimates that 70% of the video views come from such recommendations. Imagine a company like Netflix being set up at the same time and equipped with an equivalent quantity and quality of videos as Netflix; only this other company would not use AI. Its customers would be lost among the thousands of viewing options and only watch a fraction of Netflix users' views. If customers cannot find enough attention-grabbing videos, they will soon stop paying for the subscription. Netflix snowballed partly because of its ability to entice customers to binge-watch multiple videos through its AI-based recommendations[11].

Netflix goes an additional step in grabbing customer's attention by applying AI to personalized data. Using each user's preference data, Netflix can show the movie thumbnail image that the customer likes. For example, if a customer has selected movies about dogs on multiple occasions when recommending the next movie to watch, AI will choose a scene with dogs and show that scene in the movie thumbnail. As of July 2018, there were 33 million different Netflix versions according to each customer's preferences[11].

15. **Offering hyper-personalized products.** AI and other software are enabling companies to provide personalized products and services. Individual consumers are willing to pay 20% more for these products and services. Brands that offer

customized products develop a higher trust with their customers. Consumers are willing to disclose personal data in exchange for tailored products and offers.

Reduce cost

AI can help businesses lower complex processes cost by taking over several if not all the tasks involved in a process. AI's ability to analyze data to formulate predictions makes this technology different and more exciting than others. AI can reduce costs in many areas of organizations. Here are some examples:

16. **Optimize operations**. AI can learn from millions of data points collected over years of plant operations to optimize production by increasing manufacturing speeds.

17. **Reduce workers' training.** As AI takes over processes, the operation is simplified. New workers need less training when AI shares part of the work simply because they perform fewer tasks[12].

18. **Predict maintenance**. AI can predict when a particular part will go down ahead of time based on its usage, monitoring sensors including computer vision, and the piece's characteristics. This alert reduces downtime of the plant or vehicle and increases production time.

Lower risk

Computers up to now have executed the steps the programmer specified in the code. With AI, machines can learn 24 hours a day and gain new perspectives and knowledge to address complex situations full of uncertainty. AI is particularly helpful in managing risk because much of the data available today is unstructured. Structured data refers to numbers; unstructured data refers to everything else such as text, images, videos, etc. AI can derive insights from unstructured data and conclude if the tone is positive, negative, or neutral giving businesses an insight into what people are saying. As the AI algorithms continue to learn, they will detect even more complex fraud that humans could not see.

19. **Fraud detection.** After customer service and sales recommendations, threat intelligence and prevention systems are the most frequently used AI applications. AI in insurance companies, for example, can comb through data to identify networks of scam artists such as an auto repair shop, towing truck, and scoundrel working together to make fraudulent claim[7]. AI can also filter those customers who are not likely to pay back the loan they are requesting. Credit card fraud is another area where AI is popular. AI uses image processing to explore the document's visual information, but it needs a collected set of authentic and forged document images to learn.

20. **Prevent identity theft**. AI can detect phishing emails where the hacker tricks the user into providing bank account numbers and passwords by "reading" the email with natural language processing and analyzing URL, domain, website traffic, page rank, and HTTPS token, among others with machine learning[13]. Identity theft is another area where AI has been instrumental in preventing fraud. AI analyzes the person's behavior patterns and may suspect fraud if it finds significant differences. Each new transaction updates the person's patterns of behavior[13]. With Covid-19, for example, our buying patterns changed, and the existing AIs had to be fed new data.

21. **Prevent insurance claims reach litigation.** Aon Global Risk Consulting uses AI to detect the claims that are at risk of reaching attorneys and resolve them promptly to reduce cost[14]. Litigation is the highest cost in the casualty claims area at insurance companies.

22. **Reduce supply chain risk.** External events can impact the continuity of supply chains. To complicate the situation,

practitioners are also facing just-in-time goals, companies are increasingly global, and the number of international supply chain events disrupting production increases. Supply chain risk management, SCRM, aims to identify, mitigate, and monitor unexpected conditions that may disrupt the supply chain. Leaders in SCRM must make quick decisions on massive data sources, making AI a helpful technology[15].

Supply chain practitioners have used mathematical tools for years. However, some are not inclined to use AI technology simply because they are unaware of AI's potential to manage risks and uncertainty. The best alternative is to use AI accompanied by the human practitioner combining the expertise of both. To reach this point, leaders must collect data, clean it, and organize it so it can be fed to AI, a task that may not be so simple given the reluctance to share data with suppliers. Research in data security guarantees protected data sharing[15]. Blockchain is already a promising way to increase trust in data shared by supply chain partners.

Improve productivity

AI increases productivity in every industry and every function within an organization. AI eliminates the employees' routine tasks to focus on more critical aspects of their work. AI is helping people to be more accurate. Intelligent machines have helped all industries accelerate their process with a human still in control. However, leaders must be careful when selecting AI applications as some uses such as controlling and monitoring employees can hinder productivity.

23. **Knowledge workers become more productive.** AI automates mundane tasks freeing the time of knowledge workers. For example, AI solutions can automate up to 40% of the work salespeople do[16]. Deloitte, for example, developed an AI-powered program that can scan and understand complicated legal documents and extract relevant information, eliminating search time and accelerating contract

negotiation, and freeing employee time[17]. Another example is the use of AI to detect and deter security intrusions. Instead of replacing IT security professionals, the tools enhance the human capabilities needed to cope with sophisticated attacks[17].

In the healthcare industry, AI is reducing the administrative tasks of medical doctors. Google's DeepMind Health and IBM's Watson, both AIs, are already promising to take administrative duties, such as inputting information and looking for papers, away from doctors so they can have more time to devote to patients. IBM's Watson uses its natural language interface for delivering information in a way that patients can understand. Children are more open to talking about their conditions with Watson than when talking with a doctor or a nurse[18].

24. **Blue-collar workers are enabled to accomplish more**. For blue-collar workers, AI translated into increased safety at industrial companies, eliminating up to 50% of their repetitive tasks and faster installation, repair, and maintenance of complex equipment[19].

Increase employee engagement

Today's employees expect the company to treat them in a highly personalized way, know and understand their preferences, and quickly resolve their issues. Amazon and Netflix know what a person likes, Alexa answers any question nicely, and Facebook friends provide quick "likes." Employees, especially younger employees, also want to be treated well and be quickly recognized for their achievements. Just as AI can make customers happy, AI can delight employees as well, even when they know it will eliminate or change their jobs[20].

25. **Make employees' jobs easier.** A global study conducted by Coleman Parks Research surveyed employees in several

countries and found that 80% of the workers see AI as a tool that improves their work experience. Chatbots, considered friends by employees, take away dull, repetitive tasks such as answering customers' basic questions and freeing up time to help customers with more complex or anger issues. Banks have already tested this situation with ATMs, leaving cashiers to handle more complex transactions and airlines with self-service kiosks take primary check-in care. Bots transfer complex transactions or desperate customers to human employees and equip them with their history, preferences, responses, and insights. Chatbots enable employees to provide better care of the customer.

For example, an AI application that uses machine learning to analyze voice can detect if the customer is angry or happy before transferring the call. The AI chatbot can advise the employee if the customer is angry and provides information about the problem. The employee is then empowered to solve the customer's issue and will avoid attempting to cross-sell. If the customer is happy, the AI algorithm will signal the employee to try to sell more. In either case, the employee has new tools to do a better job, increasing customer retention and sales. With the means for doing a better job, employee satisfaction increases[20].

26. **Assign tasks according to employee's talents**. Nobody is good at everything, but everyone has a set of expertise. AI systems learn customers' preferences the same way AI also identifies each employee's skills. For example, in call centers, AI algorithms analyze each customer inquiry, compare it to similar calls, and send it to the employee who can handle it better. The result would be a more satisfied customer, greater employee efficiency, and increased revenue, among others[20].

27. **Enable HR to give better service to employees**. Chatbots can

take over Human Resources routine work such as answering common employee questions or communicating with employees and job candidates. These tools would free HR members time to spend on strategic projects, provide employees with more empathy, and enhance the company's culture to attract better candidates and increase retention of current employees[20].

28. **Improve training**. Employees with insufficient training may feel overwhelmed and make errors that affect customers. All employees need training on products, processes, and technology to do their job well. AI can make a significant contribution in this respect. AI algorithms with machine learning can evaluate the strengths and weaknesses of each employee and identify the soft and hard skills that need improvement. Employees will benefit from this intelligent insight because they receive the training they need and feel the company is helping to develop their careers. When employees apply new skills well, the manager can recognize and reward them, increasing employee engagement[20]. Before the arrival of AI, many employees with unique talents were hired, worked for companies, and later left without the manager ever finding out about those skills.

29. **Motivate and reward employees**. Engaged employees produce superior results. Merely paying an employee well but not providing much motivation will not work. Money is not everything. Employees today do not see a reason to stay in an organization where the salary is good, but the work environment is toxic. AI can help an employee be more effective and accomplish more, but it still needs a manager's touch to provide the praise, perks, rewards, and celebrations to make employees feel valued[20].

30. **Learning about employees' feelings**. Employees' emotions and moods may result from multiple factors and, in some

cases, lower productivity. Most of the time, supervisors have no idea of how each employee feels and are later disappointed the person did not meet the target date. AI tools such as sentiment analysis use natural language processing to determine if a text conveys positive, negative, or neutral feelings. Traditionally, companies surveyed employees to find out their level of satisfaction. These surveys would be open for days, and after a few weeks, the company would come back with a general report of the results. With sentiment analysis, the employees can express their feelings, and the tool will answer in real-time to address their issues, just like talking with another person. The person receives answers to questions and recommendations to address a problem, resulting in the person feeling understood. In addition, sentiment analysis can report the overall feelings of the workforce to management[21].

Improve marketing effectiveness

Marketing teams are adopting artificial intelligence to improve the customer experience and operational efficiency. Marketers obtain personalized, in-depth knowledge of their customers with AI tools. Marketing with AI can automate decisions based on massive data analyzed and enhanced with customer feedback and economic trends. This situation allows Marketing to communicate automatically with customers with the right message at the right time.

Artificial intelligence has three stages: (a) *mechanical* AI for automating repetitive activities, (b) *thinking* AI for analyzing data to gain new perspectives for decision-making, and (c) emotions-oriented or *feeling* AI for identifying human emotions[22]. For market research, *mechanical AI* collects data, *thinking AI* does market analysis, and *feeling AI* understands the customer. AI also plays a crucial role in developing the marketing strategy. For example, mechanical AI can be used for segment recognition, thinking AI for segment recommendation, and feeling AI for determining how well a customer belongs to the segment. Finally, mechanical AI may be used for standardization, thinking AI for personalization, and feeling AI for relations with others[22].

31. **Accelerate time to market.** Marketers today need to reformulate their strategies often to adapt to changing market conditions. Business leaders would be wise if they used a data-driven AI approach. Marketers are finding that AI has made big data finally actionable. AI uses visual analytics to automate market analysis for decision-making and even discover new markets. Marketers are also finding that they no longer need to push the product or service to customers through advertising. With AI making data manageable, Marketers can now pull prospects to buy their brand. AI gives business leaders a deeper understanding of customers and market trends but cannot yet interpret subjective experiences without humans' help. This teamwork between humans and machines eliminates the guesswork and allows a more profound knowledge of future customer behavior. Business leaders armed with AI can take companies to new market understanding levels[23].

Soon, AI will influence Marketing strategy, including business models and sales processes that will offer new options for customer services and insights into customer behavior[24]. For example, using voice or text analysis, an agent equipped with AI can detect when a customer is unhappy and transfer the call to a human.

AI can also analyze data to deliver personalized recommendations to customers[24]. In the future, retail stores may predict what customers will want and ship the order if the customer approves.

32. **Use of voice in websites**. We live in a world where chatbots

are proliferating. Advances in AI, machine learning, and natural language processing have created a generation of chatbots so human-like that people do not always realize they are talking to a machine[26]. AI-powered chatbots can talk with customers on websites, replacing the old text-based communication[25]. Using voice instead of text makes it easier to for customers to interact with the brand, obtain answers and even search for products using voice only[27].

33. **Answer clients faster.** A virtual assistant's database consists of two parts, questions and answers[26]. Virtual assistants and chatbots can assist customers on websites, online stores and automate basic customer requests. A virtual assistant gives the client short, fast, and easy-to-read answers with a solution[26]. To train a virtual assistant to understand the client and reply as a "human," developers need diverse training material to reflect the way clients speak and include the many ways clients express the same thought[26]. Chatbots and virtual assistants can access the client's information to resolve conflict situations and give personalized treatment.

34. **More and better customer surveys at a reduced cost.** AI-powered chatbots can carry conversations with clients. Understanding and communicating through natural language opens the possibility of chatbots to do more than just passively answer customers' questions. Chatbots can also ask questions and conduct formal customer surveys and interviews at a fraction of the human interviewer's cost. One of the AI tools is sentiment analysis, which analyzes texts to determine if what the person is saying is positive or negative and interprets the conversation's narrative. Chatbots equipped with sentiment analysis are cost-effective service tools for businesses[28]. Instead of having an interviewer busy writing down the answers, chatbots can process the conversation and interpret the customer's body language, detecting even minute facial gestures. Chatbots are effective interviewers

because they adapt their "personality" to the interviewee using their stored knowledge. Persons interviewed by chatbots have felt so comfortable even suggesting the chatbot become a therapist. As a result, Chatbots can become an efficient way of collecting and interpreting customers' information[28].

35. **Participate and analyze social media.** Social networks gather large amounts of data, impossible for humans to interpret. AI can help in several ways. Chatbots can hold natural language conversations to guide users to brands and services with instant messaging applications. Chatbots in social media give users a new experience. AI's predictive analytics capability can alert the Marketing department when it needs to do more live Facebook sessions or spend less on advertising, saving considerable time and money. Google recently launched new artificial intelligence algorithms that understand users' intentions and recommend the content they like. AI can write a simple report for now, but it will improve over the next few years. Several experts agree that by 2050 AIs will be able to write a best-seller. Today AI's capability is still limited, and it is not aware of human emotions. An AI application by itself cannot know if a text is funny or not. AI needs humans to learn if a text is funny or not[29].

36. **More precise video marketing.** Video marketing is more engaging than other media. YouTube uploads 500 hours of video every minute. Personalized, targeted content provokes positive responses from consumers[30]. However, manually producing and delivering customized content is practically impossible without help from AI. Marketers use AI to understand user preferences and develop relevant videos according to gender, age, geography, and hobbies. AI helps marketers to identify with precision their potential customers. With geofencing, marketers know the exact

location of each customer and can push video content to their device, such as a discount to a store in the vicinity.

Update financial institutions

Financial institutions are among the leading adopters of AI in the front and back offices[31]. The AI applications in banks are typically in customer service, fraud detection, credit assessment, risk management, internal audit, portfolio management, accounting, compliance, information security, treasury, and marketing. In addition, customers now receive one-on-one customized interaction with chatbots and virtual personal assistants[32]. However, financial institutions would be making a mistake if they limit themselves to using AI only to increase efficiency or reduce costs; they must find ways to provide new and better services. Instead, financial institutions should consider artificial intelligence as a tool to provide more valuable services to more clients[33]. Banks that do not take advantage of this opportunity will see their clients moving to other banks. Lowering costs was one of the first ways banks used artificial intelligence, but subsequent uses have brought more value to customers and higher revenues. These are the three categories of benefits that artificial intelligence has brought to banks:

37. **Cost reduction.** Machine learning has helped optimize the collection processes, eliminating inefficiencies and errors[33]. With machine learning, banks can identify which clients will pay back their loans. Allstate uses artificial intelligence chatbots to give customers complex quotes and advice. Chatbots can now automate customer service and reduce tedious manual tasks done by employees freeing bank employees to work on more critical activities. Customers talk with bots to respond to requests for banking and e-commerce[31].

38. **Income generation.** Artificial intelligence enables banks to tap on new sources of income that were previously very expensive to obtain. In the past, financial institutions focused only on large clients. With technology, smaller customers

now receive more specialized services, and the unbanked can conduct financial transactions. Some banks have applied the Amazon and Netflix idea of "if you liked this, you may be interested in this other" and have created engines to suggest which other banking product may interest their customers[33]. For example, HSBC uses artificial intelligence to give its customers personalized rewards based on their previous activity. In addition, Bank of America is experimenting with a virtual assistant, Erica, to handle finances.

39. **Prevent fraud**. Banks use machine learning to prevent fraud[33]. For example, the fraud detection PayPal uses has allowed it to reduce its fraud to just 0.32% of revenue compared to 1.32% for stores.

40. **Increased productivity.** The Commonwealth Bank of Australia uses natural language processing to interpret documents and define the next steps. Automating the understanding of regulatory documents will reduce hundreds of person-hours and increase accuracy up to 98%. RHB Banking Group uses face recognition with machine learning to give small and medium-sized enterprises the flexibility to open a bank account remotely and securely[34].

41. **Robo advisors provide financial advice**. In Wealth Management, AI-based robo advisors are making stock trading decisions and advising some clients. Robo advisors are automated financial advisors for wealth management clients and investment decisions. BlackRock has replaced part of its stock pickers with robo advisors, transferring the responsibility of asset allocation to intelligent applications to improve returns[35]. BlackRock has enabled several versions of robo advisors, each in charge of a different task. Robo advisor 1.0 automates asset allocation according to the age of the investor. Robo advisor 2.0, a bit more advanced than version 1.0, automates the risk-allocation process according to the user's risk appetite. With this version, a human investment manager may intervene to rebalance the

portfolio. Robo advisor 3.0 uses complex calculations to rebalance portfolios supervised by a human investment expert[35]. Over 60% of equity trading in the United States is algorithmic trading. The newest robo advisors are now AI-powered. The older models were simple expert systems that worked on rules. Several companies have developed robo advisors, and they are competing among themselves for the best returns.

Upgrade supply chain

Artificial intelligence is crucial in supply chain. Global supply chains have greater complexity and speed requirements while being pressured to reduce the error margin[36]. The way to meet these requirements is to use artificial intelligence with machine learning to optimize capacity planning, improve productivity, increase quality, lower costs, and increase output[36]. AI produces insights using sensors' information to do demand forecasting, customer orders, warehouse management, inventory tracking, and distribution[37]. Warehouse management and product transportation generate large amounts of data that humans without AI could not analyze at the granular level.

42. **Increase production while reducing cost.** AI will continue to play multiple Manufacturing roles, such as controlling quality, reducing materials waste, making data-driven decisions, optimizing production processes, and identifying predictive maintenance, among others[38]. Accenture estimates that by 2035, AI will increase labor productivity in Manufacturing by up to 40%. AI algorithms used in Manufacturing learn from many iterations of processes until they can predict outcomes[39]. The Manufacturing industry has always embraced new technologies. AI-based Manufacturing can be effective at making products better at less cost.

43. **Optimize inventory management.** Effective inventory

management is critical to have the correct products at the right time to fulfill orders. Inventory management problems translate into costly errors and may create bottlenecks in the supply chain. AI is highly successful for inventory management and forecasting supply and demand due to its ability to assimilate and analyze massive datasets. Additionally, AI-powered applications can predict and discover new consumer habits and forecast the seasonal market[36].

44. **Warehouse efficiency.** AI can accelerate work at the warehouse, simplify processes and resolve issues more accurately and faster than humans can. This situation translates to reducing time and warehouse staff[36]. Effective supply chains rely on an efficient warehouse to give customers a smooth journey, among other factors.

45. **Improved safety**. AI tools can analyze workplace safety data and alert about potential risks. Also, AI can identify proactive maintenance and keep warehouses safe[36]. Running a well-planned and efficient warehouse usually implies higher levels of worker and material safety.

46. **Quality control**. Machines equipped with sensors can "see" the products on the production line and spot microscopic flaws which human eyes can miss[38]. For example, defective welding can cause spots on a car's body[39]. When AI sees a defect, it marks it and sends alerts to human workers. Midea Group, a Chinese electrical appliance manufacturer, implemented AI to increase product inspection accuracy and efficiency[40].

47. **Identify areas that need attention**. There is a story about Abraham Wald, a noted mathematician, and the missing bullet holes. During World War II, the Royal Air Force consulted the brilliant statistician to recommend where the military planes needed additional armor to prevent them

from going down if shot. Too much armor meant the airplane was too heavy for flying and too little armor meant the plane would go down in flames when shot. The Royal Air Force had examined the aircraft returning from war and saw that the fuselage area had the most damage and the engine area had the fewest bullet holes. The Royal Air Force wanted to place additional armor in the fuselage, the area with the most bullet holes, but they decided to consult Abraham Wald. After examining the situation, Mr. Wald told the British not to reinforce the fuselage area, pointing out that the fuselage's damage had not stopped the planes from returning to England. Instead, Mr. Wald recommended strengthening the engine area even though it had the fewest bullet holes, pointing out that the aircraft hit in the engine never returned. The recovery rooms of hospitals have more patients with leg wounds than chest wounds. The Royal Air Force had selected only limited data simply because they had no access to the planes that had been shot down, a condition called survival bias, and reached the wrong conclusions[38].

Manufacturing leaders can also make similar false conclusions on the production floor. The products may look fine but may break down at the first use. Other products may look defective and still work well. The way we observe objects is biased. AI uses vast amounts of data to identify products with potential problems.

48. **Predictive maintenance**. AI-equipped with sensors and advanced analytics can predict when maintenance is required to prevent unplanned downtime. In the UK, 3% of working days are lost each year due to machinery failure, costing more than 180 billion pounds a year. Predictive maintenance is gaining popularity because of the considerable savings it brings[38].

49. **Robots that can learn**. Robots can perform many manufacturing jobs. The older version of robots merely followed the instructions specified in the programs. AI-powered robots are learning to do many jobs, and there is no need to program their movements[38].

Improve retail

Imagine a world where every physical and virtual store knows the best products for its customers, can offer them at a discount, always has the correct items on stock, and all the employees know which shifts to work ahead of time. If Amazon or Walmart come to mind, think about artificial intelligence, and start preparing to compete with the big players[41]. AI is doing things humans cannot, analyzing large amounts of data and freeing buyers to spend more time negotiating with vendors. Ultimately, every retailer wants to know which products to promote, what prices to charge, and what inventory to keep in the store. AI answers these questions.

50. **Managing product pricing**. Prices in stores and digital commerce are changing rapidly because of today's dynamic market. Price management relies on complex analyses and decisions. Dynamic pricing is a strategy where prices of products and services are continuously adjusted according to market demand. The pace of price changes exceeds human capabilities, but AI algorithms can manage this situation well. For example, potato chips and beer sell well before a big game, but grilled meat may not sell as well during rainy weather. These correlations may sound simple, but they are imprecise. Production and supply chains are long-term processes that are not changed easily. The sale of perishables needs precise forecasting to reduce the price and sell it quickly before the produce decomposes[42]. AI-powered pricing in an online environment plays a critical role. Unlike physical stores, where prices are not easy to change and can remain static for weeks, online stores can change prices several times a day[43]. For example, Amazon uses dynamic pricing algorithms to review the prices of

millions of products every two minutes. AI-engines are the only way to optimize pricing to survive in this highly competitive environment.

51. **Assortment management.** The correct assortment of products at the right time has always been a challenge for retailers. The physical stores have a fixed space. Adding trendy new products means displacing others. A supermarket can have over 50,000 different products and knowing which products to eliminate and which to introduce requires analyzing massive amounts of data that only AI can handle. Retailers now have a greater need to rely on AI for their assortment decisions because consumers' habits changed due to COVID-19. AI can analyze the data from before, during, and after the pandemic, combine it with other customer behavior variables to predict which items will have the highest demand[43]. This alternative is superior to the previous assortment management methods, consisting of using the last 52 weeks' history.

Retailers have a significant opportunity to improve assortment planning with AI solutions because today's retail tools are not as valuable as AI. Using AI for assortment management may be considered risky by retailers who do not use much technology, but it is a move that will pay very well. A retailer, for example, used AI with machine learning to determine the correct number of cases of blueberries to be shipped to each store but decided to temporarily move away from the system when a load of blueberries close to ripening arrived. As a result, the retailer maximized sales and minimized shrink[43].

52. **Replenishment optimization.** Determining the right time to place an order with the correct quantity for each specific product is not an easy task. Doing replenishment optimization well reduces retail companies' costs. AI also helps to identify unsold goods to avoid replenishing them.

AI-powered replenishment also includes shelf management, so shelves always look filled up, and the products with the highest sales have the most space on the shelves. For example, Marks & Spencer uses AI to stock its shelves to maximize the protection of the environment and reduce waste[42].

Walmart recently launched an AI system to detect when fruits and vegetables are about to spoil to reduce the price and place an order to the warehouse to replenish. The system, called Eden, photographs the produce with an app. The system then analyzes the images to determine the percentage of damaged fruit and how many days are left before it goes bad. The app also helps Walmart with its supply chain. Bananas turn brown quickly if transported over long distances with varying temperatures. The app suggests Walmart send the ripening bananas to stores located at a shorter distance[42].

53. **Easy checkout**. The facial recognition of AI and sensors throughout the store has permitted Amazon Go store to offer what we have wished for many years, to avoid the checkout line[42]. AI is used in stores to automate the checkout process, so customers avoid standing in line to pay[42].

54. **Personalized messages**. Chatbots and digital virtual assistants such as Alexa are helping customers to buy. AI decides which product to advertise on interactive displays based on the customer's age, gender, emotions, and body language. In some cases, customers may even interact with these displays because AI can detect body movement[42].

55. **Detecting fraud.** Customer and employee thefts account for as much as 1.3% of sales. Most of the theft happens at the storage warehouse where merchandise is received, followed by products stolen from the sales floor. Some thieves may collude with cashiers to simulate their articles registered by

the scanner or leave the products in the shopping cart and walk out with them. AI-powered cameras with image processing and recognition algorithms analyze checkout activities to warn the store manager of possible fraud. The video processed by AI can is used as evidence of theft[42].

56. **Delivery logistics**. Amazon uses small robots to carry goods to fulfill orders within a warehouse. Amazon uses AI to determine the correct inventory of each item at each warehouse, considering the season and nearby cities. When there are last-minute changes to an order, AI selects the best alternative port, estimates the arrival time, and calculates the carrier canceling probability. In addition, AI can use weather information available online to consider potential delays[42]. Distribution centers use AI to fulfill orders, plan delivery truck routes, and schedule employees for gathering the order[41].

57. **Handling delivery commitments**. Customers now expect digital commerce retailers to deliver the purchased goods on the same day or the following day at the latest. Logistics providers are using AI systems to achieve the level of efficiency expected by the customers. AI can calculate the probability of finding a truck on the needed route, its available capacity, and the cost, all without human intervention. Deutsche Post DHL Group tested a fleet of autonomous electric delivery vehicles controlled by AI that uses delivery date, customer history, price offer, weather, and traffic to plan the same-day delivery route[42].

58. **Counting store inventory**. Detecting empty shelf space or incorrectly placed products has been a time-consuming activity in stores, frequently causing employee overtime. A start-up company has developed an AI-powered robot, Tally, to control shelves. Tally moves through each aisle of physical stores, automatically scans all the shelves, and sends a

report of products that need replenishment and merchandise in the wrong location.

Digital commerce retailers face a challenge when a customer returns a product without its original packaging containing the bar code information. Often, the retailers do not know what the product is and find it difficult to update the inventory. In addition, merchandise, such as fashion and make-up, change each season, making this task even more difficult. Searching through a catalog is time-consuming, and the error rate is very high. AI-powered automatic image recognition works by recognizing the product, matching it to the catalog, and supplying the correct article number. With this information, employees can return the product to the system. However, simple image recognition without AI does not always work, especially with glossy products such as jewelry. AI with deep learning solves these situations[42].

59. **Retail accounting**. Retailers receive many paper invoices. AI can read, validate, and interpret the documents, including each invoice item and its payment terms. Digital processes are handled rapidly at a minimal cost. AI-based accounting goes a step further and can make automation proposals based on previous entries. AI can also reconcile receipts and bank information by accessing both sources, making the bank reconciliation process more reliable and with the possibility of executing it at any time. AI systems can handle accounting autonomously[42].

Advance small and medium-sized businesses

Many small to medium-sized businesses, SMBs, are not considering implementing AI thinking this technology is beyond their reach. Most of these SMBs are already using AI every day through apps and email. AI tools are available off-the-shelf with solutions for smaller-sized businesses. SMBs can keep ahead of competitors by using AI to increase sales, customer support, and cybersecurity while freeing employees' time from trivial tasks. Several of the uses of AI in SMBs may overlap with those used by larger corporations. Here are some low investment AI uses for SMBs:

60. **Targeted advertising and marketing solutions**. Facebook and Google offer AI-enabled solutions to target specific customers. SMBs can pay for these services as they go, and they can use limited budgets well by messaging only desired customers to have higher conversions. Facebook, for example, can identify the target group of potential customers among its users and use AI to find common features among their profiles to create a cluster of potential customers. This service is available to major corporations as well. What makes it so attractive to SMBs is that there is no upfront cost, and only a small amount of money is needed to reach potential customers.

61. **Increasing information security**. Cyber-attacks are everywhere, and SMBs need to protect their customers' data and themselves. Hackers are always looking for organizations with vulnerabilities to attack. Sometimes just having failed to upgrade a specific software to the next version once is enough for hackers to get into the system. Vendor companies offer solutions to detect harmful activities and protect customer credit card data. AI can accelerate the detection of potential problems by checking security data and alerts from cybersecurity firms. AI uses pattern recognition to discover harmful behavior faster than traditional cybersecurity systems. For example, AI may detect ransomware attacks early before the encryption starts, preventing many headaches. Data security practices and solutions are not optional for SMBs.

62. **Automating customer service and communication**. Customers are accustomed to communicating with chatbots from large corporations and receiving personalized product recommendations. SMBs can rent intelligent chatbots that can answer up to 30% of customer questions. Users can

develop limited chatbots in less than an hour; several videos are available on YouTube showing each step. Several SMBs are already using AI to predict customer behavior and personalize customer service. Soon, we will see AI systems using the pooled data from several large and small businesses to reduce the cost of using AI. Over the next few years, AI tools for various functions will be available.

63. **Recruiting candidates**. Google offers an AI-powered system to track candidates in small and midsize employers, called Google Hire. The application can reduce dull, time-consuming tasks to free recruiters to connect with prospects. Google Hire can review past candidates to determine if they fit new positions instead of finding new candidates each time a position is opened. Google Hire may be rented from Google and can streamline interview scheduling, search resumes, and call candidates.

64. **Reducing tedious chores**. SMBs are increasing their productivity with AI embedded in applications. QuickBooks, for example, can categorize expenses for customers with its AI. AI and other tools can eliminate repetitive tasks giving employees free time to innovate and learn new skills.

65. **Facilitating innovation.** SMBs have access to data from customers, suppliers, operations, and markets. AI can learn from this data to produce new insights, identify trends, and solve potential problems. Coupled with a workforce with reduced repetitive tasks, SMB employees may use the fresh insights to attract new forms of revenue.

Bonus benefit: Driver for digital transformation

Digital transformation leads companies to new forms of doing business where the digital world and the real-world blur. Another definition of digital transformation is the use of radical rethinking of how a business uses technology, people, culture, and processes to compete in new[40]. Companies doing digital transformation use digital technologies to create or change business processes, culture, customer experience, and even business models to compete[40]. Companies can provide new digital services, digital products, serve customers 24/7 and gain new customer insights, among other things. Digital transformation is not just implementing technologies but finding new ways to increase revenues and customers.

Digital transformation and AI are different strategies, but AI is often a part of digital transformation. When used together, one feeds the other, taking it to a new level. A robust digital transformation uses AI to disrupt its operations[40].

AI is achieving breakthroughs in businesses. This chapter reviewed how AI can improve customer experience, digital commerce, employee engagement, and productivity while decreasing cost and risk. AI is providing new ways to do marketing, supply chain, and retail, among others. The following chapter will describe the steps to build artificial intelligence in the organization. The chapter describes a complete roadmap for implementing AI. The sequence of the steps provided will help business leaders implement AI without rework. The roadmap consists of four phases and 23 steps.

AI IMPLEMENTATION ROADMAP FOR EXECUTIVES

Many companies want to implement AI because it is trendy without even knowing what is needed. AI requires a set of skills and tools used in the correct order to achieve the results. Following a roadmap for implementing AI will prevent leaders from skipping sequenced activities, resulting in rework or unsatisfactory results. This chapter addresses point 6 of this book, following a roadmap to implement AI without any delays.

> Point 6 – Following a roadmap to implement AI without any delays

The roadmap described in this chapter is from an executive viewpoint, not technical. Even with the best Information Technology department, the company will not achieve the expected results if the business side does not accomplish the 23 steps in this roadmap.

A roadmap is a visualization of a strategy. Artificial intelligence is a new technology, and the steps needed to implement it are not the same as those of other technology projects. A roadmap for implementing AI specifies the steps required, mitigates challenges, and prevents delays by having all prerequisites done on time. The AI implementation requires upper management, an AI leader, an AI sponsor, IT, business managers, Risk, Legal, Compliance, and several vendors. An AI implementation roadmap consists of four main parts: (a) understanding AI, (b) preparing for AI, (c) implementing AI, and (d) reaping the rewards, as shown in figure 6.

Roadmap for Implementing Artificial Intelligence

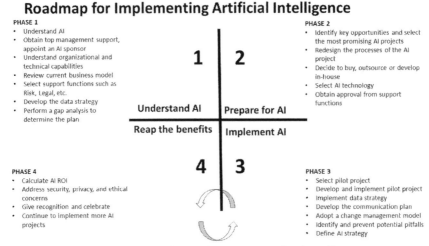

PHASE 1
- Understand AI
- Obtain top management support, appoint an AI sponsor
- Understand organizational and technical capabilities
- Review current business model
- Select support functions such as Risk, Legal, etc.
- Develop the data strategy
- Perform a gap analysis to determine the plan

PHASE 2
- Identify key opportunities and select the most promising AI projects
- Redesign the processes of the AI project
- Decide to buy, outsource or develop in-house
- Select AI technology
- Obtain approval from support functions

PHASE 4
- Calculate AI ROI
- Address security, privacy, and ethical concerns
- Give recognition and celebrate
- Continue to implement more AI projects

PHASE 3
- Select pilot project
- Develop and implement pilot project
- Implement data strategy
- Develop the communication plan
- Adopt a change management model
- Identify and prevent potential pitfalls
- Define AI strategy

1 Understand AI **2** Prepare for AI

4 Reap the benefits **3** Implement AI

Figure 6. Roadmap for implementing artificial intelligence

Phase 1 – Understanding AI

The first phase consists of understanding AI at the conceptual level; there is no need to learn all the technical aspects. This book provides a comprehensive view of AI at a strategic level. Each person has their idea of AI, be everyone understands all the AI's myths and realities described in chapter 1. There are plenty of available resources to learn about AI at a strategic level. Suppose you wished to learn more about a particular topic related to AI, for example, chatbots. Multiple online resources are available such as Udacity, Coursera, and courses from some universities and companies on the topic of chatbots. Some courses are free. Learning about how to use AI in the business is not a one-time endeavor. AI and the rest of the emerging technologies continue to evolve, bringing new opportunities for organizations.

Obtain top management support

Help the CEO and the management team to visualize the future with AI. Obtaining leadership support is crucial. Multiple academic studies point to the need of having executive support for an innovative initiative; artificial intelligence is no exception. Without the backing from the top, change initiatives may start, advance a few steps, and invariably die. Any change requires the employee from the organization to invest time and effort to learn how to work under the new scheme. Employees are already overworked. If they see top management is indifferent to the change and only a few persons trying to push for the change, their answer will be "not now, maybe later," and there will never be enough time for later.

When preparing to present the case for AI to top executives in an organization, the first step is to tie it with crucial company objectives. Show how the AI benefits can impact the executive's business objectives. Top management will be open to new technology if they can visualize how it will make it easier to achieve their goals. Providing plenty of examples from other companies helps to paint a clear picture. One of the primary uses of AI is to improve the customer experience. Communicate the AI initiative in terms of the business benefits, mention AI at the end. Describe why the change is needed and why their support is needed.

Whet the appetite of senior leaders for AI by describing how other companies are using AI. The fear of missing out, FOMO, is a powerful motivator. Executives do not want to feel their friends in other companies are leaving them behind. Do not allow executives to embrace AI because it sounds innovative; ensure AI is always used to fulfill business objectives. Learning what other companies are doing, even from different industries, can spark ideas about their company's potential uses. Using the ideas from other sectors may be particularly valuable because a proven practice somewhere else may be innovative in their industry.

Explain how AI can solve specific current problems. Most executives want to see a rate of return for every proposal. Defining the benefits of a project with new technology may not always be possible, but showing what AI can and cannot do may help executives understand the benefits of AI. If possible, the benefits AI will provide to each of the company's functions should be included. Helping directors understand how the organization can compete when computers read, write, and understand conversations may provide them with an edge.

The last part of obtaining top management is to make a compelling case. Philosophers advise using three approaches to make a persuasive argument: credibility, feeling, and logic (numbers). First, describe the current situation: cost, resources needed, errors, complaints, slow processes, negative impact on customers and employees, among others. The second step describes life using AI: customer satisfaction, reduced cycle time, cost and time reduction, and contribution to strategic company goals[1].

Before the presentation to the executives, identify who has the power. Typically, more than one executive will need to sponsor the AI initiative. Research each executive's business goals and try to show how AI can help. Try to meet one-on-one with each of the top decision-makers before the AI presentation to convince them of the benefits. Rehearse the presentation; every meeting with the CEO is a critical event in a work career. Identify the metrics and priorities used to measure the performance of the CEO. Explain how the AI proposal will allow the CEO to reach the personal metrics and priorities. Try to anticipate any questions upper management may have and bring the material to cover them. Before the CEO meeting, try to meet with a few influential leaders to convince them to support the initiative.

Once top leadership supports using AI to achieve key business objectives, ask them to communicate their support to the organization. One way may be to make a short video where the executive states the reasons to support AI projects and uploading it to the intranet or sending it via WhatsApp for all employees to see. The executives must emphasize AI will augment the current staff, not eliminate them. Request management to appoint an AI leader, preferably from the business side, not from IT. Some boards may be hesitant to invest. Give executives an idea of the possible levels of investment required to prepare for the following steps. If the executives are not open to supporting AI, they may need more insights into AI's benefits. Proceed with the next steps only after senior management is committed to at least exploring AI. This phase is a good time to appoint an AI leader for the company, preferably with a business background.

The rest of the organization will also need evangelization. People have a natural fear of losing their jobs when new technologies arrive. Leaders must explain to employees that AI is more likely to help them carry out their assignments by eliminating tedious tasks rather than displacing them. Pointing out that training will help them transition, and an AI expert will be at hand to answer any questions will help ease some anxiety. Another issue employees and management may have with AI is transparency$_2$. If the AI models are incorrect or fed incomplete data, these applications may be harmful to the company. Individuals are less likely to trust an AI algorithm if they do not understand how it works. A meeting with the heads of the Risk, Legal, and Compliance areas to explain AI and how it may affect their disciplines will help gain their support. The involvement of these areas at later stages of the AI roadmap will be necessary to ensure transparency and trust.

In this initial part of the AI implementation, IT must review its technical capabilities, software, and AI talent. The funds may not yet be approved to buy the equipment, but this is the right time to review vendors without buying. Identifying the AI skills needed and sharing the list with Human Resources to begin recruiting employees with these skills is also part of this phase.

Data acquisition can never start too soon. An essential activity in this phase is developing a data strategy to define the tools, rules, and processes to manage, analyze and use business data. A significant component of this strategy is making the organization aware of gathering data to explore insights. IT should inventory existing data and locations and plan to collect and organize the data in a central repository. The data strategy should also include assigning owners or stewards to each piece of information. Each data steward will later define who is authorized to read or update the data under their care.

Another critical activity in this phase is considering new digital business and operating models. Is the current business model traditional, omnichannel, or ecosystem? Frequently, the business model may overlap with another model. A meeting with senior executives to explain each model's benefits and obtain their commitment to move to an omnichannel or ecosystem business model would be desirable at this stage. During the meeting, evaluate the company's place in existing networks and define how to become part of other networks to acquire more value and data. Implementing artificial intelligence in an isolated way is valid for initial experimentation. Organizations reap the AI benefits when they accompany the technology with organizational changes. Staying in a traditional business model while adopting AI will result in only marginal gains. Moving the organization to an omnichannel or ecosystem business model will amplify AI benefits. Implementing an effective AI needs reviewing processes to eliminate bottlenecks. There is not much gain if the total cycle time remains the same after implementing AI because the transaction had to wait for someone.

Developing the data strategy

Data is a prerequisite to artificial intelligence. Without data, no AI is possible. Launching an artificial intelligence initiative with insufficient data means potentially spending over 50% of the AI initiative's time and effort in collecting, integrating, and organizing the data to obtain no results. A data strategy is necessary from the start of the AI initiative, even before developing an AI strategy.

A data strategy is needed as a guide to obtaining the required data and should include the models, policies, standards, and rules to govern the gathering, storing, and consolidating data. The data strategy is an approach to allow persons across the company to find and work with the data[3]. Ensure senior leaders are aware of the importance of data and support its use for serving the customers and operating the business. They play a crucial role in achieving a culture of data, so everybody knows about the power of data.

The first step to develop a data strategy is to review the business strategy. Use data to deliver on the strategic priorities and to answer the critical business questions. Many use cases are available, but it is preferable to select the three to five projects that will contribute the most to the company's priorities[4]. The use cases may take some time to show their results, but the organization still needs to see results to believe in the value of data. Pick one to three quick wins to prove the value of data and obtain support for the strategic data use cases.

Once the business strategy is clear, the next step is to define the data needed to achieve those goals with the organization's strategic objectives. Consider structured data such as Excel spreadsheets and unstructured data such as text. Next, evaluate if the plans can be achieved with internal data or will external data be needed. External data can be obtained through social media, websites, or purchased. The following step is to evaluate whether the organization already has the data required. If not, find ways to obtain it[4].

Leaders need to define data governance, infrastructure, skills, and the implementation plan to complete the data strategy. The first step is to institute data governance. Clean data does not come easily; organizations must initially clean the data and keep it at the same quality level when the data is updated. Data used for analytics and AI is a critical asset. If anyone tampers with the data, the company may suffer from insights leading to poor decisions. Data quality, data security, privacy, and ownership of data become critical issues. For each piece of data, leaders must appoint a person responsible for ensuring the data is accurate, complete, and updated. These persons are called data owners or stewards, and they make sure only authorized persons can view or update the data. All vital data must be stored securely[4].
Concurrently with defining a data governance scheme, the

technology must be made available. The storage and management of data require technology infrastructure. Processing the data to extract insights will need machine learning or deep learning in more sophisticated cases. Communicating the results in a meaningful way will require reporting and data visualization tools4.

Neural networks consume large amounts of training data, and producing the labeled data may be expensive. For example, an AI algorithm may need a million colon cancer scans before it can "read" and diagnose new images correctly. If a trained physician needs six minutes on average to diagnose and label an image, and the physician earns $50 an hour, the training set's cost would be $50 million. A way to avoid the enormous cost is to make available open data sources with data that several medical diagnosis networks can use.

To complement the above points, leaders must ensure the correct data skills are available. Lack of data skills is often the most significant barrier preventing the full use of data. Each organization must evaluate if the skills needed to deliver results with data are available by either training in-house personnel or hiring new persons. If the idea is to work with external skills, define how the potential providers.

The last step in defining the data strategy is to develop and implement a plan. The plan must include a list of critical activities, the order of execution, who will be responsible for each action, and when. The plan should include the business needs to support the new data culture on a broader scope.

Executives need to cultivate a data culture in the organization. Leaders must nurture curiosity about the new ways that working with data may bring efficiencies and improve results. Data managers should offer data literacy programs that include data management and analytics concepts such as data governance, data modeling, statistics, and visualization. As users learn to apply the data tools, they will increase the use of data self-service. Communicating the data strategy implementation's progress and value will accelerate embedding a data culture in the organization[3].

This roadmap includes the activities needed to implement AI. For a more personalized approach, a gap analysis may help. First, to do a gap analysis, determine the future state and what the organization will look like once it uses AI. Ask what the future customer service will look like, what new insights the company will have, and how operations will improve. Once the future state is well-defined, proceed to describe the present state. Many people make the mistake of defining first the current state and then the future state. The gap analysis does not work well this way. When describing the present state, include the good and the bad; it is not a school exam. Finally, the third step is to do a gap analysis is the action plan needed to move from the present state to the future state.

Phase 2 – Preparing for AI

The second phase of the AI roadmap is to prepare. At this stage, we have top leadership support, an AI leader, and the organization is already gathering and organizing data. The first step is to define use cases and select a pilot project. The use cases are the initial golden opportunities the business has to use AI. IT should not be the only area responsible for implementing AI. Leaders must work closely with IT engineers but must envision new ways to use the emerging technology to serve customers better and attain a competitive advantage. Either leaving this responsibility to the business alone or IT alone will not work. Both parties are needed, one knows about the industry, and the other knows about the technology, and through cooperation, they will uncover the opportunities AI offers. Firms need collaboration among several areas and ideas from different industries and apply design thinking techniques to invent the future. Once the AI concepts are clear, the possibilities of using AI techniques in an organization will start to become apparent.

Implementing a pilot project is critical to proving to the organization the benefits of AI. The pilot project is a small project to meet a key business goal. The pilot project's objective is to prove that AI is a valuable technology that can achieve business goals possible in ways that were not possible before. The pilot project should be small enough not to require much investment or resources and should not depend on other projects or events that may delay the AI project. Often there is competitive pressure to do a particular project without defining its business goals simply because leaders fear missing out on the opportunity. Ensure the success of the pilot project will contribute to the business. AI projects are executing processes in new ways, and the full results may be difficult to predict. Typically, AI projects may result in greater agility, improved customer experience, and reduced cost. At the end of the project, the team should present the results to upper management and the organization. This approach is the most eloquent way to communicate that AI works for the organization.

Once the pilot project concludes, the next step is to scale it until it goes into production. Scaling a project deserves attention because, on average, only 25% of AI proof of concepts reach the production environment$_5$. Prototype first but scale fast. There are two ways to move an AI pilot project to production. One is by incremental improvement, where the pilot project's activities continue while the scope widens incrementally. For example, if the pilot project involved a chatbot, the training with the customers' possible questions and answers should continue, periodically releasing new versions. Gradually the bot will get better at answering questions and will be able to answer more questions as the training continued.

The second way to scale an AI project is by applying the lessons from one or more pilot projects to other larger projects. After an organization developed a chatbot capable of handling a few transactions and has proved how the chatbot implementation has saved time and cost, the next step will be to take the same chatbot and train it to service a business application$_5$.

The data strategy was developed in phase one of the AI roadmap. In phase two, it is time to implement the data strategy. The person leading the data initiative, typically called Chief Data Officer, should determine the data vital to the enterprise, collect it, clean it, organize it, and store it in a central repository. The data leader must make the business aware of the importance of critical data and obtain their commitment to protecting the data. Naming data owners or stewards for each piece of data is necessary to protect the data. Ensure plenty of quality data is available. AI needs enormous amounts of clean, accurate data so artificial intelligence can learn, correlate patterns and trends[6]. Most organizations have a data quality problem. Before embarking on AI, expect to spend considerable time and resources to clean up the data. Many of the company's current systems do not produce data fit for analytics or AI. Another problem is that data resulting from one system is either transformed manually or by another application. The definition of the same type of data may vary in each application, or some of the data may be in silos.

Many years ago, my company purchased another company. I was responsible for combining the invoicing data for both companies. I thought it would be a simple task, re-formatting the data to adapt to our invoicing files and do quality checks to ensure clean data; what could go wrong? As we started to transfer records, errors in the data began to show up. Fine, I thought, let's get the data cleaned up, and we can finish. We spent the entire weekend working 12 hours each day to clean up the data. The message of the story is not to expect your company's data to be clean and ready to be used for AI. Even some company areas distrust the data from other functions. Always validate current data before embarking on the AI application.

Fortunately, functional data quality tools exist in the market. To improve data in your organization will require asking these questions:

- Who has access to specific data (organizational level, confidentiality)?
- How can data be accessed (read-only, modify or delete)?
- What is the origin of the data?
- What are the quality standards for data (data completeness

and accuracy)?

- How will the data be used?[6].

Capture plenty of the correct data and store it in an organized manner. Ensure the data covers all situations and has no biases. Augment datasets by purchasing external data. Consider implementing data governance to ensure all critical data has a steward and all incoming data meets quality standards.

The next activity in phase two of the roadmap is developing a communication plan. The leader must create a communications plan to reach all. A helpful format is to define a table specifying each of the company's functions as columns and levels within the organization as rows. For each cell, determine the type of message and the means to communicate the message. Once the table is complete, the leader will have a clear idea of gaps and resolve them.

Internal social media and collaboration platforms are the fastest and most effective means to help employees understand and commit to the change. Social media opens the possibility for people to ask questions, share ideas and express doubts and concerns. A video sent via WhatsApp will probably be seen and remembered by more stakeholders than a boring email. People look at their cell phones over 90 times per day. Identify employee influencers to start online conversations on the change initiative, exerting peer pressure to convince others, and creating a virtual community around the change[7]. Internal social media allows people to establish a dialogue between the communicator and the employees. Communicate using the intranet. Most employees view the intranet daily. Placing attractive text and videos on the change is another way to get the message across.

After communicating the change to the organization, speak with employees three or more levels down from the CEO. Probably, the entire message about the initiative did not reach them. This exercise will show how the communications plan will need to be modified. Nobody has yet witnessed a significant change initiative where employees complain that there was too much communication.

When developing the initiative communications, make sure the language is clear and appropriate. Craft several messages to reach all levels of employees. The communication must convey the scope of the change to clear any worries. Avoid using jargon or technical terms; the employees will not understand and will not bother to ask. The messages should also explain the change and why it is needed. If people do not know why a change is necessary, they will not cooperate.

The next step in the roadmap is to adopt a change management model to prevent employee resistance from overthrowing the AI initiative. Over 200 change models exist in the market today. Select the model with the best fit for the organization. A compelling vision of the change must be defined and communicated in several ways to the organization. Refer to chapter 2 for more details of change management.

Potential pitfalls when implementing AI

AI brings many benefits, but its implementation may present several challenges. Over 40% of AI initiatives have failed. The leading cause of failure is insufficient, clean data. Companies must have robust data security, data governance, and data organization processes to meet AI's needs. Companies can dedicate over half the AI project to preparing the data. A data strategy rolled out from the start of the AI initiative can mitigate the problem.

Another major cause of the failure of AI projects is opaque AI. AI with machine learning and deep learning can quickly become black boxes. When people cannot understand why the computer is making a specific recommendation, the immediate reaction is to distrust it and stop using it. Mistrusting the AI algorithms or blindly trusting them may result in failure. Leaders should ensure AI results are explainable and transparent and the data fed to the system was robust and clean.

The lack of staff expertise is another cause of AI project failure. If the AI algorithms cannot be purchased or leased, the leaders must outsource talent or develop in-house. The current wave of AI usage is still recent, so that AI skills may be non-existent to the organization. Ensure the right skills are in place and outsource AI expertise to supplement. Other causes of potential problems in the AI implementation are:

1. Implementing AI projects that have nothing to do with the core business objectives. AI is a superb technology, but opportunities will be lost if it does not address strategic business goals[8].
2. Executing AI in siloes, limiting the technology to modify only small parts of each process. Disconnected technologies, systems not integrated, resulting in difficulty in achieving a helpful user experience. Just as in the dot.com era, having an AI initiative removed from the core business is doomed for failure.
3. ack of clean data, especially customer information necessary to feed the AI algorithms. Leaders are failing to address the organizational resistance to change. If the employees feel threatened by AI, even the best plans will fail.
4. Thinking AI is just a technology to be used in projects. Failing to consider how the business and operating models need to change will lead to wasted investments and effort.
5. Unrealistic expectations, thinking AI, will immediately increase profits.
6. Lack of success metrics and lack of business objectives. If success is a matter of opinion, the project is doomed[9].

Once we complete the preparations, we are ready to define the AI strategy. Many leaders want to develop their AI strategy from the beginning of the initiative before understanding and preparing for AI. This approach is a mistake. A general going into battle does not develop the strategy to win the conflict without first knowing the resources he has, the battlefield conditions, and an estimate of the enemy's situation. The same is true with artificial intelligence.

An artificial intelligence strategy defines how the business will use AI to succeed. The AI strategy should be unique and different for each organization. To formulate an AI strategy, follow these steps as shown in figure 7:

Developing an Artificial Intelligence Strategy

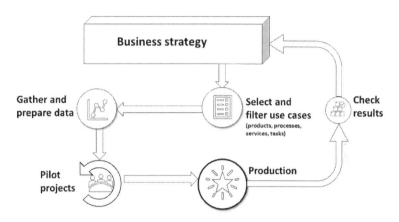

Figure 7. Developing an artificial intelligence strategy

1. Review the business strategy and business challenges. If the business strategy is out of date, management should meet to formulate a new plan. Review key business priorities for any changes.

2. Once you know where the company wants to go, ask what problems it wants to solve and how AI can deliver the strategic goals[10]. Look for opportunities to digitalize products and services. If the business manufactures products, ask how sensors may be applied to generate data, use the data to feed AI applications and develop new digital products to be sold, similar to the services Schneider Electrical added to its elevators. If the company sells a service, evaluate how to make the services smarter with AI[11].

3. Look at the critical business processes paying additional attention to customer-facing processes. Consider automating each process with applications, tools, and AI to make it run smoothly without human intervention, similar to

how Ant Group can grant loans in less than a minute.

4. Identify repetitive business tasks and consider automating those tasks. Also, identify critical manufacturing processes and evaluate automating those.

5. For each of the use cases, link it to a strategic goal. If the use case has no connection with a strategic objective, discard it.

6. From the list of use cases, select two or three quick wins to prove AI's value from the start.

7. If the AI algorithms do not have transparency and are not ethical, they will never be successful. AI, machine learning, and facial recognition, among other technologies, invade people's privacy and may not be well received. Partial or biased data may mean discrimination. Examine each AI project for possible biases, legal implications, and privacy invasion[10].

The AI strategy needs a data strategy. Without data, AI cannot learn. Verify each AI use case to ensure sufficient data is available. Also, ask if the correct data is available to meet all the AI priorities. If the data needed is not at hand, define how the organization can obtain the data through additional data collection methods or access third-party data[10].

Phase 3 – Implementing AI

Now that we have completed the understanding and preparation phases for AI, we are ready to implement it. Phases 3 and 4 consist of selecting, implementing AI projects, and delivering the results. This phase should be executed in a loop. These are the steps recommended to choose the key AI opportunities in an organization:

1. Identify critical AI use cases. The first step is to review company strategies, goals, and unique challenges to identify potential AI solutions[11]. Using AI to solve a problem that is not important to the business is a waste of resources. AI

helps corporations in many ways. Rather than focusing on an AI technique, for example, implementing a chatbot, focus on the business problem to be solved.

2. Expand the list of potential AI projects. Explore the many ways AI can help the business achieve its strategic goals[11]. Consider projects that make your products more intelligent, such as installing sensors to monitor conditions (like Schneider Electric's sensor installation to alert breakdowns ahead of time). Review business processes to automate the steps and make the process more intelligent by applying AI to handle decision-making points. AI is also useful for automating repetitive tasks[11]. With these two steps, companies will have a list of potential AI projects.

3. Select the best projects. At this point, leaders must be lasered-focused on customer value. Some managers may press to get their projects done, but those projects may not be critical to the customers and the business. The 80/20 rule applies to this list. 20% of the projects will yield 80% of the benefits. Review each project in the list and determine if it has a link to the business goals. If it is not clear how the AI project will help the business grow, discard it. For the remaining items on the list, review if sufficient data is available. Data is the number one obstacle to implementing AI. Define the objectives of the rest of the business cases. Is the project solving a business-critical problem, reduce cost, reduce employee turnover, etc. If a project has no clear goal, it is only nice to have, discard the project.

4. Define the selected projects. Define success metrics, owners, data needed, legal implications, technology infrastructure, skills, and implementation challenges for each project remaining on the list. Avoid stating a vague objective such as increasing sales by 12%. Sales can go up or down by many factors, and it will take an act of faith to say that an increase in sales was only due to the AI project. A better alternative is to go down one level in the objectives hierarchy and select a more specific objective, such as increasing visits to online channels by 10%. Instead of setting a goal to improve the

customer experience, track the on-time delivery of the product or service accuracy and set a goal to increase their accuracy by 10%. If the project involves implementing a chatbot, an appropriate objective would be to grow the first-call resolution by 15% or reduce abandon rates by 20%.

5. Narrow down the list to a few strategic choices. For the resulting list, set up a graph and plot each use case as a point, as shown in figure 8. The x-axis is an estimate of the amount to be invested in the project, and the y-axis is the estimated benefits. Develop first those projects yielding the highest returns with the lowest investment. The number of projects to be developed concurrently will depend on the resources available and their benefits. The goal at this point is to have the top one to three strategic use cases. For small businesses, consider only one project. Working on 10 to 15 AI concurrent use cases as pilot projects is a recipe for disaster. Do not throw away the list of projects not chosen.

Filtering Use Cases

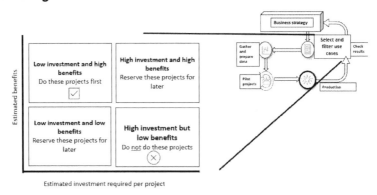

Figure 8. Filtering use cases

6. Identify one or two AI "quick wins." From the use case list, pick one or two AI quick wins. These projects will show the organization the value of AI and convince them to support larger projects.

AI technology used without changing core processes will only bring limited value. The processes where AI is being implemented must be redesigned to eliminate non-value-added steps to permit a frictionless execution. If only part of an existing process is automated, the project benefits may be marginal because the bottlenecks will continue. Ant Group did not achieve the economies of scale by automating only some of the steps of their processes. Redesign the process to eliminate non-value-added steps and take advantage of the characteristics of AI. An excellent way to find the bottlenecks in a process is to briefly form a team consisting of one person from each of the areas involved with the process, map the process together and then identify those steps that do not add any value to the business nor to the customer. The next step is for the team to develop the new process map without unnecessary steps and take advantage of the latest technology. Mapping the current state and future states with a multifunctional team is the basis of Lean methodology for process redesign.

Consider buying first, outsourcing second, and developing in-house last to acquire the artificial intelligence for each project. Recent developments have increased AI use in all industries, creating a need for new skills that are not always plentiful. Once the pilot project starts, most leaders want to develop the application in-house. Giving in to this temptation may be a mistake.

The first option when developing an AI should be to buy or rent first. If the project is not providing a unique competitive advantage to the company, look for products with artificial intelligence built-in that can be purchased and installed. Some technology companies offer AI built-in products as a service; the product is "rented" instead of purchased. Buying or renting AI software is the fastest way to show the company some of the benefits of AI. Many software solutions already have AI built-in and can be purchased directly. The fact that a solution exists does not mean it is the right business solution; each solution must be evaluated$_{12}$.

The second option to develop an AI is outsourcing it if buying or renting are not options. Today's connected world offers crowdsourcing and multiple resources available for doing any task. Developing artificial intelligence applications through a third party is an excellent alternative to finish the project faster. Outsource AI applications that provide a competitive advantage.

The last option for an AI project is to develop it in-house. Only as a last resource consider developing AI applications in-house. If the AI project's objective is to achieve a unique level of competitiveness, assess the AI skills available in the organization and consider hiring skills and training the staff. If acquiring the new skills is manageable, consider developing the project with in-house resources. Before committing to developing a project in-house, assess the availability of the data. Most enterprises have plenty of data but not the correct data type[12].

Once the use cases are selected, the next step is to define the technology needed. AI consists of several technologies such as machine learning, natural language processes, speech translation, image recognition, and pattern recognition. With these technologies, many applications, including chatbots and virtual personal assistants, may be developed. See figure 9. Some of these technologies may be re-used in several applications. For example, a chatbot used for customer service can also be used for internal financial or Manufacturing systems to make them more friendly.

Artificial Intelligence Technologies

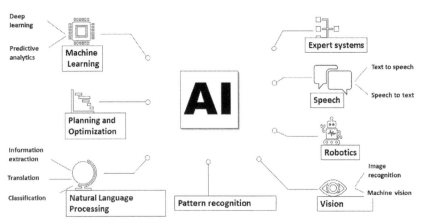

Figure 9. Artificial intelligence technologies

AI also requires data science, programming languages, logic, governance, cognitive learning theory, and algorithms. Not all the skills need to be in-house; consider a hybrid approach. When building an AI algorithm in-house, the team members will need to develop a model and classify the data into two categories: training the AI and testing the AI. IT must have the right tools and platforms so the AI algorithm can start learning from the data.

The last step in this third phase of the roadmap is to obtain approval from the Risk, Compliance, and Legal areas for the AI projects during the development stage. AI is different from other business applications because it can learn, and the results may be difficult to control. AI applications learn and evolve as they continue to learn, auditability and traceability become challenging. Stakeholders from Risk, Legal, and Compliance may be hesitant to approve AI applications if they do not fully understand them. Understanding the AI applications goes beyond the technology risks. Help persons from Risk, Legal, and Compliance to understand the customer journey to see the potential benefits and become aware of the points where risks could arise and how to mitigate them. Financial Institutions are subject to government regulations that request personal data use and explain the assumptions used in fully automated decisions.

Phase 4 – Reaping the benefits of AI

Phase 4 of the AI implementation roadmap is crucial. The first step is to realize the benefits of AI projects implemented to prove that AI works and that it is safe to invest in additional AI projects. Establishing AI transparency is necessary to proceed with more projects. The last step in reaping AI's benefits is recognizing and celebrating successes so people will want to do more projects. Organizations should then go back to phase 3 and implement additional AI projects.

After finishing any project, the team must prove the benefits. Unfortunately, many companies skip this step and just continue to implement other AI projects. Not calculating and communicating the benefits is a mistake that leads to a lack of trust in the results. The situation is akin to a bank lending money to a person; the person uses the money to implement a project but never bothers to return the loan to the bank. Instead, the person returns to the bank for a new loan. You can imagine what the bank will say.

AI projects are not like typical IT projects. AI projects take longer to return the investment. Some frequent problems are gathering, organizing, and cleaning the data and developing and training the algorithms. A clear business case also helps. To calculate the ROI of an AI project, compare the costs and benefits over five years. Since AI projects are more expensive, consider all costs and benefits over five years. If you include only the first year to calculate the return, the figure will probably be negative. The cost calculation should consist of storage, gathering, aggregating, standardizing, and analyzing data from multiple systems. The cost also should include deploying, tuning, and maintaining the AI model and tools that explain how AI came up with any conclusion. Form multifunctional teams and people with domain knowledge of the application. Also include the cost of buying the AI or outsourcing and the cost of adopting agile practices. The cost of educating others in the organization and managing the change.

The benefits of an AI project will vary according to each project. The most common benefits are improvements to organizational efficiencies, such as time to execute a process and answer calls, accuracy, and response time. Other common benefits are reducing customer churn and abandoned calls, increasing revenue and leads, and enhancing customer experience. A third common category of benefits is risk reduction and detection.

A successful way to measure the results of AI projects is to form a multifunctional team from the start of the project consisting of one person from each area affected by the project to keep track of the project's effort, resources, and results. This team will also be responsible for ensuring the business conditions are available to realize the benefits. AI applications do not produce a predictable outcome, such as the case in traditional systems. AI applications are based on decision models that may rely on a probabilistic model or the data fed. This characteristic means AI can solve problems through pattern identification, but it also means the performance is harder to predict.

New security, privacy, and ethical concerns
AI opens excellent possibilities for doing business in the digital age, but it also brings new concerns such as keeping the data safe from cyberattacks or having transparent algorithms. Major technology companies such as Google and Microsoft invest resources to reduce algorithmic bias, and Facebook addresses fake news and dangerous posts. All companies need to safeguard the information of their customers, employees, and suppliers. Investors no longer tolerate security breaches compromising critical information and demand the CEO's termination when an information attack happens[13].

A frictionless environment where enterprises can scale up with no cost or constraints may have a downside of rapidly spread bias, aggression, and false information. This challenge will require a new type of response from digital companies. These actions can overcome the problems:

- Develop/refine data privacy, security, and ethics policies.
- Request approval from customers before sharing their data.
- Algorithms and logic must be transparent so people can trust them.
- The responsibility always rests with humans, not robots. Humans should make all critical decisions.
- AI should never endanger humans.
- Work with employees to identify areas where job loss is imminent to encourage them to train with new AI-era skills.
- Enforce clear data use agreements with vendors[6].

In addition to these steps, leaders should also address broader issues. Corporations using AI have found some complications such as biases in data, cybersecurity attacks on data, and algorithms inciting potentially dangerous situations forcing them to act. Like any new technology, AI has its good and bad points. Companies need to learn about the potential negative aspects of AI and take steps to manage them without damaging others.

Bias in training data feeding AI. The quality of the algorithm results depends on the quality of the data and assumptions previously selected. A common type of algorithmic bias occurs when the input data does not represent the population correctly. In July 2020, in the middle of the COVID-19 pandemic, college entrance exams could not be held because of infection risk. The UK decided to use an AI algorithm instead of a college entrance exam. The AI took the students' existing grades and tracked records at their schools. The result was the AI gave bright students from minority and low-income neighborhoods lower scores simply because they went to schools that, on average, had lower scores. Wealthier students attending expensive schools were given higher grades by the AI[14]. There was no ill intention in feeding the AI algorithms, but the dataset's lack of screening resulted in an uproar. A philosophical problem complicating this situation is that what appears as a bias to one person may be perceived as fair by others.

Another source of bias is mislabeled data. Part of the data preparation process is a group of persons labeling each photo with a description. Labeled images are already available worldwide to train AIs. The problem is that many of these labels may have some biases. For example, a picture showing a woman with a man in a hospital may either be labeled as "a woman and a man" or as "a nurse and a doctor." In 2017, computer experts at Princeton found that labels such as the latter one resulted in having "woman" or "female" being associated with teaching and the humanities while "man" or "male" were associated with math and engineering.

Algorithmic bias is a critical topic, but it is still in its infancy. Removing bias is difficult, but managers must understand how to select the dataset from a transparent source and ensure the data represents the problem to be solved[13]. Algorithmic bias may result from the way data is coded, collected, and used to train AI.

Security attacks on the data. Data is the new electricity, and more information means more possibilities of a cyberattack. The number of cyberattacks is increasing. A hacker attack occurs every 39 seconds, and 95% of cybersecurity breaches are due to human error[15]. Many major companies such as Equifax, Marriott and Microsoft, and even governments have received hacking attacks. The most significant breach in history occurred in 2013 when hackers stole three billion Yahoo accounts. Digital thieves obtained a copy of names, birth dates, phone numbers, passwords, and even the security questions and answers used to reset lost users' passwords. Yahoo executives initially thought one billion Yahoo accounts had been stolen, but forensic research proved all three billion accounts were affected. In 2016 a hacking group in Eastern Europe offered Yahoo's information for sale for $300,000. Three spammers purchased the information[16].

The case of Equifax in 2017 received wide publicity. It exemplifies how hackers use any vulnerability to attack. Hackers in 2017 did not intend to hit Equifax only. The hackers attacked multiple sites for a specific vulnerability that allowed for remote code execution. Equifax was the only one with this vulnerability. The hackers then installed programs to see, change and delete data and even created new accounts using more than 50 databases. The attackers were able to keep their attack concealed for 76 days. The CEO had to resign and blamed the vulnerability on a single employee for failing to update software. To make matters worse, Equifax executives mismanaged the situation by delaying the communications for over a month, sold company shares for $2 million while investors remained unaware[13].

Privacy limits must be re-defined. Imagine walking into a store, and a sales rep offers to help. The sales rep knows all your past purchases and the number of items viewed and for how long, and using that knowledge, recommends items for you. Would you feel comfortable? Or would you prefer to continue receiving recommendations via digital means, even knowing the algorithms know our history? A new task for companies in the AI age is to define the limits between personalization and privacy. An airline discovered that a loyal customer, an older adult who flew first class, liked when the airline attendants remembered how she likes her coffee but felt uncomfortable when the same attendant remembered her dog's name, Winston. AI is uncovering new social issues which we must address.

Many online sites capture large amounts of data about the habits and interests of each user. The sites sell this information to advertisers, presenting the user with targeting ads and tempting, hard-to-res resist promotions. Another use of the information may be to manipulate the behavior of users for political purposes.

Filtering questionable material. Not all attacks involve stealing information. The use of videos showing war atrocities, for example, has been banned from social media. Even with the ban, some users leaked a few violent and spine-chilling videos on social media. In some cases, a user calls law enforcement, and the site removes the footage before it is shared too many times. A few years ago, social media companies hired persons to filter suspicious videos manually, but the results were disastrous. After two weeks on the job watching horrifying and inflammatory videos, the persons reviewing them had to quit and seek mental help. Social media companies have since relied on AI to filter disturbing content. Before applying AI, YouTube flagged and removed only 8% of the videos containing extreme violence. With machine learning, YouTube deleted more than half of violent videos before reaching ten views[4]. Social media is under pressure to detect and remove offensive videos because sponsors are quick to pull their advertising dollars, fearing perceived as connected with terrorism.

AI in military weapons. The use of AI in the military has been controversial, and leaders have made several agreements to avoid its use, but there are always loopholes[17]. AI could help military tactics. AI can already do facial recognition and release thousands of low-cost small drones to attack the enemy. With facial recognition, the drones would hit the persons targeted and leave the rest unharmed. The drones would only need to carry small ammunition doses since they would shoot from a very short distance. Leaders will need to continue with the agreements to avoid using AI for military purposes.

Algorithms inciting negativity. Google, Amazon, and Facebook use personalized algorithms to show us what we like, increasing views, purchases, and personal engagement. Having algorithms search information to sell us products or ideas that we may like has a dark side. Algorithms partly fueled conspiracy theories in 2020 and 2021. Extremists set up groups in social media with thousands of members, and algorithms will recommend even more events, groups, and information that keeps users engaged but, unfortunately, may incite violence and boost the conspiracies[18]. AI can make our lives better, but it can also drive negative situations to the extreme if social media does not curb it.

Algorithms can accelerate the communication of any news, including fake news. An example was the anti-vaccination movement that spread rapidly. Unfortunately, much fake news in social media such as Facebook, WhatsApp, and Twitter is accepted readily by many people without questioning its validity. Digital networks reach more people than traditional media[13]. Social media companies have already put additional AI algorithms to detect fake news before they travel too widely. Still, even today, they are not able to identify all fake news.

When users sign up for a social media account, they provide personal information. Users' posts on social media reveal much more information such as family, personal interests, and beliefs. All of this data is stored and used to target personalized advertising. Companies may also share or sell personal data with other companies. Connectivity with others means there is no more control once the information is in their hands[13]. Facebook users placed information on their walls. Facebook sold this information to Cambridge Analytica.

Another example of dubious magnifying material is the use of YouTube's AI-powered "Up Next" feature. Users of YouTube upload 500 hours every minute. AI must make recommendations using a continually changing dataset, which is not the case for Netflix nor Spotify[19]. YouTube's AI solution to recommend other videos to users consists of two parts. The first part reviews the user's YouTube history, and the second part assigns a score to each video. AI applications measure success if the user watches the videos, a valid measure for the system but not so beneficial for the user. This setup could push questionable content to be seen by more people. More views of this type of content would be recommended more times by the AI system[19].

Distrust in the use of the technology. The results of AI solutions may change drastically even with minor changes in their input data. For example, changing just a few pixels of an input image can change the image to a completely different one. Even a person looking at the previous and new pictures cannot tell the difference. Unfortunately, this situation leads to uncertainty and distrust of AI applications. The concerns increase in the case of face recognition. If only a few pixels change the photo of a person's face, will the algorithm still identify the same person or someone else? If a stop road sign is changed, for example, attaching post-its on strategic locations, will the driverless car still recognize it as a stop sign?

Today's tools powered with AI can edit images, videos, and soundtracks that appear factual but are fakes. Advanced equipment and sophisticated forensic skills are required to recognize a fake video; ordinary tools or a person's inspection are still unable to detect if the video is real or not. As AI evolves, new tools such as blockchain will reach the market to tell us the difference.

The AI applications must be transparent to be accepted by regulators, clients, and employees. Transparency consists of seven principles, awareness, access, accountability, explanation, data provenance, auditability, and validation[20]. Awareness means developers should know their application's possible biases and the harm the biases may cause. Regulators should encourage mechanisms to enable questioning and give access to persons affected negatively by the algorithms. Companies will be held responsible for decisions made by AI applications they use, even if they cannot explain the results. Companies should keep a description of the data collection process and an analysis of its potential biases. Store all models, algorithms, and data to facilitate future audits. A good idea is to perform routine tests to determine if the model generates any harmful results[20].

AI uses neural networks, which are layers of neurons interconnected so the algorithm can learn. The neural network encodes the training examples and extrapolates them to estimate data results, not in the training samples. The problem happens when a human wants to know why the network generated a specific outcome. In the past, with conventional programs, the person would locate the code segment responsible for the result and modify it if needed. People do not see any program logic in a neural network, just unintelligible, gigantic data. One of the key research areas today is having explainable AI[17].

Having a transparent AI is necessary to satisfy regulators, assure customers their data is used correctly, and employees that the AI is doing the job correctly. Developers must monitor AI because it can amplify biases. For example, Google Translate at one point would translate an English text such as "he is a nurse, she is a doctor" into Hungarian where there are no gendered pronouns, and the translation back to English will say "she is a nurse, he is a doctor"[20]. Using AI as a packaged solution does not diminish the need to verify the results, especially in sensitive cases. For example, having AI look for potential signs of mental health problems to provide help is one thing, but to use the same system to deny employment or health insurance is another[20].

When the results of the AI projects are achieved, provide recognition and celebrate the success. Recognition is like money; no amount is sufficient. Whenever there is a significant change, employees always ask, "What's in it for me?" All change communications should mention the reward and recognition given to the persons participating in the change. Reward programs drive rapid behavior change. An effective way to change fast is to include the new way of working as goals for the employees' annual performance. Instead of waiting until year-end to evaluate the results, managers should do frequent check-ins. Shifting long-term to short-term accountability allows managers and employees to focus on the behaviors needed at that moment, becoming more agile[7].

Monetary rewards are always well-received, but non-financial rewards or recognition is a longer-lasting motivator. Non-financial rewards may be meaningful work, career planning, training, or a manager praising an employee in front of the team, specifying what the employee did right and the benefits obtained. A bonus or a salary increase may make an employee happy for a couple of days, but well-given recognition will have a more lasting effect[7]. If a team has already adopted the AI change, take a photo, and write a short paragraph describing their success story. Publish the picture and the text on multiple media. Employees are always curious to see pictures of their peers.

Project teams often work hard and achieve success only to have their efforts go unnoticed. Invariably, the next time the manager asks team members to work hard, they will hesitate to commit. Recognition does not have to be complicated or expensive; all employees want their managers to notice and publicly recognize their hard work. Here are some ways managers may recognize the team members results:

1. Hold an ice cream party to announce the success of the team.
2. Cover the desks of the team members with balloons.
3. Send them thank-you notes written by hand.
4. Invite team members to a nice lunch or dinner.
5. Present the "state of the department" (like the State of the Union) to communicate the accomplishments, paying tribute to each successful team.
6. Arrange for the team to present their results to upper management.
7. Establish a space, physical or virtual, to place photos, posters, messages, etc., to recognize project progress, showing the persons who participate.
8. Email the entire company with a picture of the team, the team members' names, and a brief success story of what they accomplished.
9. Give recognition certificates in front of the staff and their supervisors.
10. Provide time off when the team worked overtime.

Once part four of the roadmap is complete, go to part three to implement additional AI projects.

In this chapter, we reviewed the roadmap to implement artificial intelligence. The first part of the roadmap consists of first understanding AI, obtaining top management approval, designating an AI leader, review the business model, and developing the data strategy. Once the AI preparation is complete, the next step is finding key opportunities. In this phase, we refine the use case list, develop a strategy of buy, outsource, or develop in-house, select the AI technologies, prevent pitfalls, and obtain Legal, Compliance, and Risk approval. The last part of the roadmap should prove AI's benefits, ensure the organization trusts AI, provide additional training, and recognize the successes.

The next and final chapter concludes the book with a summary of each chapter and the leaders' responsibilities to implement artificial intelligence, including visualizing new business opportunities made possible with AI.

WINNING WITH AI: A SUMMARY

Times change, and companies must change to survive and thrive. The internet profoundly changed businesses, created new jobs, new companies, and increased market value by billions of dollars. During the 1990s, most business executives did not suspect the potential of the internet in their organizations. Many did not even bother to learn how to use it. By the late 1990s, some companies set up an independent division to open a dot.com. Kmart, in 1999, invested heavily in bluelight.com but failed like many other companies because they did not integrate the portal with the rest of the business[1]. A siloed approach did not work for new internet start-ups and will not work with artificial intelligence. The evidence is clear, most of the dot.com organizations closed. The companies that profited from the internet used it to enhance and advance their business strategies, such as taking orders over it, opening new customer service channels, and adopting omnichannel business models[1]. Leaders must understand how AI can make a business successful, and it is not just about implementing technology.

Leaders' new responsibilities

Leaders have several new responsibilities when the organization implements AI. Among these responsibilities are upgrading the business model, eliminating process bottlenecks, and changing the organization's culture to accept the new changes. One responsibility stands above the others, visualizing new opportunities to apply AI, the seventh and last point of this book.

> Point 7 - Visualizing new business opportunities made possible with AI

We are creating a new world, and AI is one of the key enablers. Businesses can now operate, serve customers and venture into new markets in ways that were not possible before. The first step to reach the new future is for the leaders to envision it. Defining new ways to operate and compete may seem daunting. Follow these steps described in this book to come up with new ideas:

1. Redesign core processes to find new opportunities. A multifunctional team must map each core process to identify and eliminate bottlenecks. When redesigning the new process, the team will be able to pinpoint new ways of doing business. Ensure several team members are familiar with the new AI capabilities as described in this book.
2. Upgrade to a digital business model such as omnichannel or ecosystem. Meeting the requirements for these new business models will provide several opportunities to change ways are done.
3. Search for successful ways other companies in the same industry have used AI, evaluate, and implement those ideas. For even more creative ways of imagining the future, examine successful stories from other industries and apply the ideas to your own company. Some changes may be needed to adapt the ideas, but you will be the first in your industry to come up with these new ways of competing. Review chapter 3 to identify profitable ways to use AI and select the most promising ones for your business.
4. Leaders are responsible for defining a vision for the business, but not all the ideas on achieving the vision must come from the leaders themselves. Leaders can involve other persons from within and outside the organization to brainstorm ideas and select the most valuable ones. These are some of the events and activities leaders can leverage to come up with new, brilliant ideas on using AI to compete:
    a. Workshops where a group of persons meets to generate creative ideas about a specific challenge or opportunity.
    b. Structured design sessions using different techniques, including divergent thinking and physical prototyping. These sessions can last from a few hours to weeks.
    c. Competition to leverage the innate desire to win to

motivate a group of people to generate valuable ideas. The competition can be among individuals or small teams.

d. Hackathons or innovation days are an event that lasts one or two days to develop prototypes of business plans, new products or services, customer experiences or any other idea. The participants form small groups to work in parallel on a goal or a problem, and at the end, each one proposes their ideas. Winners receive prizes.

e. Ideas or jam challenges where ideas are collected from a large community through a tool or a website that allows participants to contribute, discuss and even vote digitally. The idea jam can last from a few days to a few weeks. The idea jam event helps discover previously unrecognized opportunities with teams geographically dispersed.

f. Internal investment capital program where employees present their ideas about products or services to an executive committee who select one or more ideas and provide money for their implementation.

g. Personal projects or allowing employees to spend up to 20% of their time on an innovation project. Google and 3M allow their employees to spend between 10% and 20% of their time working on a personal project relevant to the organization. This method uses the personal motivation that each employee can bring and allows them to be creative.

Leaders must learn the basics of AI and look for ways to use this technology in several areas of the company. AI will significantly impact businesses, even more than the effect of the internet, and leaders have the golden opportunity to shape their companies' future.

AI technology is easy to implement; the most challenging work will be changing processes, skills, organizational culture, business model. Moving to a digital business model like omnichannel or ecosystem will not be easy, but it will be an innovation with a profound impact. Leadership should come from all levels. It only takes one IT analyst failing to install a software patch to open the system to hackers, but it takes an organization working together to achieve the new future. There is no need for all employees to become data scientists; each has a role to play.

The AI age brings many changes and challenges for business leaders. Companies embracing AI to bring new ways of serving customers and operating internal processes, but at the same time, the business must continue to meet its strategic goals. Above all these challenges, leaders first adapt their mindsets to use AI's potential and, most importantly, inspire employees to grow into the new AI era.

Employees know AI is coming and will eliminate or change most jobs, possibly their own. They know that they will have to train to continue being employable. Secretly the employees fear that they will not master the new work and lose their jobs. Leaders must help employees overcome their fears of AI and its consequences. Line managers need to train employees to work with data and AI_2. Instead of only supervising other employees, managers now will design, oversee and execute AI algorithms.

Above everything else, leaders must inspire others to reach the AI vision. AI represents a significant change in the organization, and managers must use the correct leadership type to succeed. When the pace of change was slow, as was the case in the 20th Century, transactional, the administration worked well. Managers laid out the objectives, and if the employees met the goals, the managers would award salary raises and bonuses. Since changes happened slowly, managers could define the objectives, and the employee worked on delivering the results.

The AI-powered digital visions that companies define lead the organization to new, promising situations but full of uncertainty. In today's changing world, organizations need transformational leadership. Leaders use transformational leadership to motivate employees through inspiration, persuasion, and motivation to achieve a clear vision. Leaders need to create and communicate a vision and inspire and motivate employees to achieve more than previously thought possible$_3$.

Seven points business leaders don't know about competing with AI

The seven points presented in this book will guide leaders to use AI to succeed in their business. Figure 10 shows the seven points leaders often do not know to become successful with AI:

The seven points business leaders don´t know about competing with AI

1. Enabling the organization to use AI.

2. Eliminating core processes bottlenecks.

3. Upgrading to an omnichannel or ecosystem business model.

4. Learning about AI successes in your industry.

5. Applying AI successful uses from other industries to your business.

6. Following a roadmap for implementing AI without delays.

7. Visualizing new business opportunities made possible with AI.

Figure 10. The seven points business leaders don't know about competing with AI

Leaders must manage change's strategic and operational aspects to inspire the organization to implement the new vision. Here is a summary of the business, process, organization, and technology changes leaders must accomplish to be successful with AI:

Chapter 1 – Amazing opportunities everywhere!

The first chapter describes the exciting world we live in where the prices of energy, water, bandwidth, computing power, and storage are dropping by ten-fold or more over the next few years. This drastically changing scenario opens many countless opportunities, many of which AI plays a key role.

Artificial intelligence is the computer science branch that simulates human intelligence[4]. What makes AI different from other technologies is learning from data and developing new insights humans had not reached before. AI can sense, hear and act, allowing it to enhance the customer experience in ways that were impossible before. These new capabilities change the way businesses compete. Companies can now offer personalized customer service 24/7 and set up promotions for select customers at the time when they are most open to buying. In the back office, AI can predict when a piece of equipment will need correct maintenance, reduce cost and risk, increase efficiency, and prevent fraud.

Artificial intelligence is the most promising technology today, but leaders will inevitably encounter skeptics. Obtaining upper management support for the AI initiative is crucial. Focus on how AI can meet its goals, not just on implementing the technology for its own sake. Point out AI will bring an additional US 30 trillion by 2030 to the world economy, increasing GDP by 1.2% per year.

Chapter 2 – Upgrading the company to the 21st Century

Traditional businesses will struggle in the age of AI, while 21st Century companies will reach new levels of success. This chapter describes the characteristics of the AI era as background for the framework to move the company to the current age. The framework consists of three parts. The first part is to prepare the organization to work with AI by learning about its uses and developing a culture open to change. The second part of the framework removes fat from processes to provide a clean highway where AI gives fast responses to customers. The third and last part of the framework examines today's business models and provides a path to upgrade to a digital business model, either an omnichannel or ecosystem. This framework includes three of the seven points leaders must know to compete with AI:

Point 1 – Enabling the organization to use AI
Point 2 – Eliminating core processes bottlenecks
Point 3 – Upgrading to an omnichannel or ecosystem business model

Chapter 3 – 65 profitable ways to implement artificial intelligence

The third chapter describes 65 ways to use AI to obtain benefits. The ideas are grouped into eight categories: customer experience, digital commerce, increase sales and productivity, reduce cost and risk, improve employee engagement, and examples from various industries. The purpose of describing these diverse examples is to trigger ideas on the uses of AI. Leaders should select three to five opportunities to make the most significant contribution to the company's goals. The most common AI applications today are in customer service, recommending other products, and fraud detection. This chapter addresses two of the seven points for leaders:

Point 4 – Learning about AI successes in your industry
Point 5 – Applying AI successful uses from other industries to your business

Chapter 4 – AI implementation roadmap for executives

The fourth chapter describes a detailed roadmap for executives to implement AI to win in today's world. The roadmap consists of 23 steps in four stages: understanding AI, preparing for AI, implementing AI, and reaping the rewards. The first stage, understanding AI, focuses on the business capabilities, developing a data strategy, the technology itself, obtaining support from top management to start testing AI to meet the organization's goals. During the second stage, preparing for AI, the leaders must identify and evaluate critical opportunities to select the AI project with the highest potential. A multifunctional team should review and redesign the process involved with the pilot project using a lean methodology to obtain better results. In this stage, the IT team should select the AI technology and buy, outsource or develop the AI application in-house.

The third and fourth stages are iterative. During the third stage, the organization should select, develop and implement the AI pilot project. The data strategy should be implemented in this stage. The third stage is an excellent time to implement the communication plan and adopt a change management model to overcome employee resistance. The end of the third stage is the appropriate time to define an AI strategy because, at this point, the leaders know enough about the business and the AI technology to make the correct decisions of its use. During the fourth stage, the AI team needs to calculate the AI rate of return to prove that AI benefits exist. When the AI benefits are verified, the team should celebrate. AI brings security, privacy, and ethical issues which the organization must address. At the end of the fourth stage, return to stage three. This chapter addresses point 6 for leaders:

Point 6 – Following a roadmap to implement AI without any delays.

Chapter 5 – Winning with AI: A summary
The final chapter summarizes each part of the other chapters. The massive changes and opportunities AI brings to businesses raise new challenges for its leaders. Influential leaders must identify the strategic uses of AI in their companies while adapting the organization, processes, and business models to new ways of competitiveness. Using AI with a digital business model and fat-free processes with a workforce open to changes will result in companies providing new customer experience types and higher profitability

levels. The final chapter describes the seventh point:

Point 7 – Visualizing new business opportunities made possible with AI

AI is the way to a brighter future

Implementing AI technology is the simple part. The most challenging part will be changing the organization, adopting a digital business model, accumulating data, and changing the culture to have a digital operating model. The difference between successful and unsuccessful artificial intelligence projects is the organizations' business strategy, not only the technology itself[1].

Using AI is imperative. In less than ten years, artificial intelligence will be widespread across all organizations and embedded in our culture to the point of not calling it AI anymore.

As corporations consistently apply AI to gain and retain customers, they will engage in new ways, accelerate innovation and compete with digital companies[1]. If companies do not implement AI now, they will be at risk soon. Leaders do not have the luxury of waiting to see how others adapt AI; it is crucial to start preparing for a future with AI applications. Organizations that delay this decision may not catch up later to competitors who leveraged AI opportunities[5].

Being AI-driven means making thousands of decisions based on AI insights to run the business better than competitors. As experts from McKinsey say, "The size of benefits for those who move early into these technologies will build up in later years at the expense of firms with limited or no adoption"[5].

Now it is your turn.

Would you like to have a copy of a chart "43 Ways to Obtain Business Value through AI Technologies"? Just send your email to mbasualdo@accelencia.com.

Did you find this book helpful? Please leave an Amazon review.

COMMON AI TERMS

The most common artificial intelligence-related terms are:

Agile philosophy. Agile is a new way to manage projects and changes in general. Agile requires a new mindset for achieving business agility. In project management, instead of waiting until having all the requirements before starting coding, the team members define part of the requirements and start coding. In agile, the development is iterative. Cross-functional teams define requirements and solutions, delivering value faster with higher quality.

Algorithms. A series of instructions or rules to solve a problem. Algorithms can perform calculations, automated tasks, and process data$_1$.

Alpha Go. A computer program based on AI plays the board game Go. In 2016, Alpha Go beat Go champion Lee Sedol.

Analytics. The discovery and interpretation of insightful patterns in data.

Artificial intelligence. Artificial intelligence consists of computer systems that perform tasks usually done by humans, such as visual and speech recognition, decision-making, and translating texts$_2$.

Augmented reality. A technology that overlays a computer-generated image on a picture, providing a composite view.

Autonomous vehicle. A vehicle capable of moving itself with little or no human input by sensing its environment.

Artificial general intelligence. Artificial general intelligence, AGI, is a system that has consciousness and can think independently, like humans[3]. AGI does not yet exist, and several experts debate whether this technology will exist in our lifetime.

Bot. A program usually on the internet capable of interacting with users.

Chatbot. A computer program powered by AI that simulates human conversation either through voice or chat.

Clustering. The task of grouping objects with similar characteristics. Clustering is a statistics technique.

Data set. A data set is a collection of data commonly represented in tabular form.

Deep learning. Deep learning is a part of machine learning and consists of algorithms similar to human neural networks[3]. Deep learning uses multiple layers to extract features from data, such as images, to "learn" from it. Deep learning can be supervised or unsupervised.

DeepMind. A company founded in 2010 developed the AI-based AlphaGo program using deep learning and defeated the Go world champion in 2016.

Ethics of artificial intelligence. The ethics of AI refers to the ethical quality of its insights and its impact on people. Lack of transparency with AI tools means humans do not know how AI reached an insight. AI is only as ethical as the data it consumes.

Expert systems. Expert systems are computer applications designed to solve complex problems, such as finding why a manufacturing plant went down. Experts' knowledge is captured in the system using debugging aids to walk any user through a problem to find a solution even if the expert is not available. However, expert systems do not perform well in all areas. Expert systems capture knowledge and rules to solve problems through a procedural code, but they do not learn. For example, an expert system cannot train enough to recognize the difference between a muffin and a Chihuahua[4].

Image recognition. Image recognition or computer vision is a subset of artificial intelligence where computers can understand digital images or videos. For example, searching Google Photos with the keyword "animals" will result in pictures with animals[3].

Intelligent virtual assistant. A software agent that helps users by performing tasks. Sometimes virtual assistants are referred to as chatbots. Examples of smart virtual assistants are Alexa and Siri.

Lazy learning. Part of machine learning where the system waits until it receives a query to process training data. The opposite is eager learning, where the system learns before it is needed[1].

Machine learning. Machine learning is a part of artificial intelligence. Machine learning systems learn automatically. With this knowledge, machine learning can identify intricate patterns among massive data sets. Examples of machine learning are the recommendations made by Amazon, YouTube, or Netflix[3]. Machine learning can be supervised (most common), unsupervised, and reinforced.

Narrow artificial intelligence. Narrow or weak AI can carry out specific tasks but does not know anything else. The artificial intelligence available today is narrow[5].

Natural language processing. Natural language processing, NLP, is a part of artificial intelligence that deals with computers and human language[3]. Speech recognition is the ability of machines to hear and recognize words. NLP is the machine's ability to listen to conversations and understand their meaning to respond with the correct action. Virtual assistants such as Siri, Cortana, or Alexa use NLP. When a person speaks to Alexa or Siri and the machine answers, the artificial intelligence is hearing the words, translating them to text, processing the text, and translating the text back to voice.

Neural networks. Neural nets are part of machine learning, where a computer learns to perform a task by analyzing labeled data sets. For example, for artificial intelligence to learn to recognize a coffee mug, the system must review many coffee mug images to distinguish the coffee mug from other objects. Neural networks somewhat resemble a human brain because it consists of millions of interconnected layers of processing nodes. The information flows from one layer to another.

Open AI. Open AI organizations are dedicated to research AI to develop a friendly way for the world to benefit. OpenAI refers to OpenAI LP, a profit organization, and its parent OpenAI Inc, a non-profit organization.

Pattern recognition. A term used in computer science to identify patterns from data such as speech, images, or stream[6].

Predictive analytics. A variety of statistical techniques to analyze past and current data to make predictions.

Python. A programming language released in 1991 used for artificial intelligence.

R programming language. A programming language used by statisticians and data miners for data analysis and artificial intelligence.

Reinforcement learning. An area of machine learning alongside supervised learning and unsupervised learning. The focus is on finding a balance between exploring new knowledge and the exploitation of current knowledge. Reinforced learning teaches an autonomous vehicle to learn to park itself, among other applications.

Robotic process automation, RPA. RPA is a type of business process automation technology based on software. RPA watches users perform routine tasks and translate these tasks to its system. Experts currently debate whether RPA is part of artificial intelligence or not.

Robotics. The design and construction of machines to perform tasks done by humans. Robotics combines an interdisciplinary brand of science and engineering that uses artificial intelligence, sensory feedback, and electronics.

Speech recognition. Speech recognition is part of artificial intelligence and refers to the process of "hearing" words and translating those words to text[3].

Supervised learning. Supervised learning is a type of machine learning that maps an input to an output-based example. Supervised learning may use either classification or regression. Diagnostics, customer retention, image analysis, and identity fraud detections use the classification part of supervised learning. Forecasting multiple aspects of life, from weather to life expectancy, relies on regression.

Types of Machine Learning

Supervised Learning	Unsupervised Learning	Reinforcement Learning
Maps an input to an output-based example. Examples of supervised learning are:	Unsupervised learning helps find previously unknown patterns in data sets. Examples are:	Learning with no supervisor, only rewards. Examples are:
• Predicting house prices • Diagnostics • Predicting unhappy customers • Image analysis • Identity fraud • Forecasting weather • Forecasting life expectancy	• Finding customer segment • Exploratory purposes • Face recognition • Image recognition • Recommendation systems • Targeting marketing	• Parking • Controller optimization • Motion planning • Dynamic planning • Game AI • Robot navigation

Unsupervised learning. Unsupervised learning is a type of learning that helps find previously unknown patterns in data sets with the help of labels[1]. Unsupervised learning uses clustering for targeting marketing and customer segmentation. It also uses techniques that reduce the number of input variables in a dataset. Examples of dimensionality reduction are big data visualization and determining if an email is spam.

REFERENCES

Introduction

[1]Wiltz, C. (2016, June 1). How Google's AI beat champions at the world's most complex game: in an advancement no one thought was coming for decades, Google has developed an artificial intelligence capable of beating champion-level players at go. *Design News, 71*(6).

[2]Balakrishnan, T. & Chui, M. (2020). The state of AI in 2020. *McKinsey.* Retrieved from https://www.mckinsey.com/business-functions/mckinsey-analytics/our-insights/global-survey-the-state-of-ai-in-2020

[3]Diorio. S. (2020). Realizing the growth potential of AI. *Forbes.* Retrieved from https://www.forbes.com/sites/forbesinsights/2020/05/08/realizing-the-growth-potential-of-ai/?sh=343540e633f3

Chapter 1

[1]Iansiti, M., & Lakhani, K. R. (2020). Competing in the Age of AI: Strategy and Leadership when Algorithms and Networks Run the World. *Harvard Business Review Press.*

[2]Bughin, J., Seong, J., Manyika, J., Chui, M. & Joshi, R. (2018). Note from AI frontier: Modeling the impact of AI on the world economy. *McKinsey Global Institute.* Retrieved from https://www.mckinsey.com/featured-insights/artificial-intelligence/notes-from-the-ai-frontier-modeling-the-impact-of-ai-on-the-world-economy

[3]Ramirez, V. B. (2018). Why the Future is Arriving Faster Than You Think: Grab on to an Ever Changing World. *Teachers Matter, 40*, 18–21.

[4]Diamandis, P. [Singularity University] (2019, November 2). SU Global Summit 2019, Keynote [Video]. YouTube. https://www.youtube.com/watch?v=ZeHoFuOtUp8&t=1905s

[5]El Namaki, M. S. S. (2020). From Product to Function: The Strategic Artificial Intelligence Shift. *Scholedge International Journal of Business Policy & Governance, 7*(2), 19–24.

[6]Sako, M. (2020). Artificial Intelligence and the Future of Professional Work: Considering the implications of the influence of artificial intelligence given previous industrial revolutions. *Communications of the ACM, 63*(4), 25–27.

[7]Arlotto, P. (2020, February 1). Artificial intelligence: 5 realities for financial leaders: The first step in a healthcare organization's artificial intelligence strategy should be education. *Healthcare Financial Management, 74*(2), 32.

[8]Garwood, M. (2018). Ready or Not, Here Comes AI. *Broadcasting & Cable, 148*(17), 14–N.PAG.

[9]Yao, M., Jia, M. & Zhou, A. (2018). *Applied Artificial Intelligence: A Handbook for Business Leaders*. TOPBOTS Inc.

[10]Chowdry, A. (2018). Artificial intelligence to create 58 million new jobs by 2022, says report. Forbes. Retrieved from https://www.forbes.com/sites/amitchowdhry/2018/09/18/artificial-intelligence-to-create-58-million-new-jobs-by-2022-says-report/?sh=146786f44d4b

[11]Ealey, E. (n.d.) Five myths about artificial intelligence: Know your science fact from fiction. Retrieved from https://www.ttec.com/articles/five-myths-about-artificial-intelligence

[12]Hippold, S. (2020). Six AI myths debunked. Smarter with Gartner. Retrieved from https://www.gartner.com/smarterwithgartner/ai-myths-debunked/

[13]Patrizio, A. (2020). 8 misleading AI myths – and the realities behind them. InfoWorld. Retrieved from https://www.infoworld.com/article/3514577/8-misleading-ai-myths-and-the-realities-behind-them.html

[14]Anayoha, R. (2017). The history of artificial intelligence. Harvard University. Retrieved from http://sitn.hms.harvard.edu/flash/2017/history-artificial-intelligence/

[15]Koch, C. (2016). How the Computer Beat the Go Player. Scientific American Mind, 27(4), 20–23. https://doi.org/10.1038/scientificamericanmind0716-20

[16]Sahota, N., & Ashley, M. (2020). How Artificial Intelligence Will Change Our Lives. *Saturday Evening Post, 292*(4), 48.

[17]Jabr, F. (2012). Does Self-Awareness Require a Complex Brain? *Scientific American*. Retrieved from https://blogs.scientificamerican.com/brainwaves/does-self-awareness-require-a-complex-brain/#:~:text=Scientists%20differ%20on%20the%20difference,that%20one%20is%20aware%20of

[18]Talty, S. (2018). What will our society look like when artificial intelligence is everywhere? Smithsonian Magazine. Retrieved from https://www.smithsonianmag.com/innovation/artificial-intelligence-future-scenarios-180968403/

[19]Louhiainen, L. (2018). *Artificial Intelligence: 101 things you must know today about our future*. [Kindle] Retrieved from https://www.amazon.com.mx/dp/B079JXCVGS/ref=dp-kindle-redirect?_encoding=UTF8&btkr=1

[20]Haenlein, M., & Kaplan, A. (2019). A Brief History of Artificial Intelligence: On the Past, Present, and Future of Artificial Intelligence. *California Management Review, 61*(4), 5–14.

[21]Schlenoff, D. C. (2017). The motor vehicle, 2017. Scientific American. Retrieved from https://www.scientificamerican.com/article/the-motor-vehicle-1917-slide-show/

[22]Fleming, M. (2020). AI Is Changing Work -- and Leaders Need to Adapt. *Harvard*

Business Review Digital Articles, 2–5.

[23]BasuMallick, C. (2019). 3 effective leadership skills you need in the age of AI. *HR Technologist*. Retrieved from https://www.hrtechnologist.com/author/chiradeep-basumallick/

[24]Whiting, K. (2020). These are the top 10 job skills for tomorrow – and how long it takes to learn them. *World Economic Forum*. Retrieved from https://www.weforum.org/agenda/2020/10/top-10-work-skills-of-tomorrow-how-long-it-takes-to-learn-them/

[25]Diorio. S. (2020). Realizing the growth potential of AI. *Forbes*. Retrieved from https://www.forbes.com/sites/forbesinsights/2020/05/08/realizing-the-growth-potential-of-ai/?sh=343540e633f3

Chapter 2

[1]Iansiti, M., & Lakhani, K. R. (2020). Competing in the Age of AI: Strategy and Leadership when Algorithms and Networks Run the World. *Harvard Business Review Press*.

[2]Sans, N. (2020). Five ways to prepare your company for digital transformation. *Forbes*. Retrieved from https://www.forbes.com/sites/forbesbusinesscouncil/2020/06/04/five-ways-to-prepare-your-company-for-digital-transformation/?sh=2686de2a7f68

[3]Lichtenthaler, U. (2020). Beyond artificial intelligence: why companies need to go the extra step. *Journal of Business Strategy, 41*(1), 19–26.

[4]Weill, P. & Woerner, S. L. (2018). *What's Your Digital Business Model? Six Questions to Help you Build the Next-Generation Enterprise*. Boston: Harvard Business Review Press.

[5]Rigorous testing. (n.d.). Retrieved from https://www.google.com/search/howsearchworks/mission/users/

[6]Clayton, S. J. (2021). An Agile Approach to Change Management. *Harvard Business Review Digital Articles*, 2–5.

[7]Alqatawenh, A. (2018). Transformational leadership style and its relationship with change management. Business: Theory and Practice, 19: 17-24

[8]Corporate Operating Models in the Age of AI: An Interview with Marco Iansiti. (2020). *Research Technology Management, 63*(5), 12–19.

[9]Ansong, E. & Boateng, R. (2019). Surviving in the digital era – business models of digital enterprises in a developing economy. *Digital Policy, Regulation and governance, 21*(2), 164-178.

[10]Fafhih, N., Henten, A., Foroudi, P. (2018). A framework for business model with strategic innovation in ICT firms: The importance of information. *The Bottom Line,* (1), 16.

[11]Diamandis, P. [Singularity University] (2019, November 2). SU Global Summit 2019, Keynote [Video]. YouTube. https://www.youtube.com/watch?v=ZeHoFuOtUp8&t=1905s

[12]Boojihawon, D. K. & Ngoasong, Z. M. (2018). Emerging digital business models in developing economies: The case of Cameroon. *Strategic Change, 27*(2), 129-

137.

[13]Valdez-De-Leon, O. (2019). How to develop a digital Ecosystem: A Practical Framework. *Technology Innovation Management Review*, (9), 8.

[14]Ungvarsky, J. (2020). Omnichannel. *Salem Press Encyclopedia*.

Chapter 3

[1]Sahota, N., & Ashley, M. (2020). How Artificial Intelligence Will Change Our Lives. *Saturday Evening Post, 292*(4), 48.

[2]Agrawal, A., & Kirkland, R. (2018). The economics of artificial intelligence. *McKinsey Quarterly, 3*, 102–108.

[3]Thiel, W. (n.d.). The role of AI in customer experience. Retrieved from https://www.pointillist.com/blog/role-of-ai-in-customer-experience/

[4]Clark, S. (2020). 4 ways AI is improving the customer experience. *CMS Wire.* Retrieved from https://www.cmswire.com/customer-experience/4-ways-that-ai-is-improving-the-customer-experience/

[5]Four Key Steps To Enhance Customer Experience With Artificial Intelligence. (2018, November 17). *Business World.*

[6]IDC Survey Finds Artificial Intelligence Adoption Being Driven by Improved Customer Experience, Greater Employee Efficiency, and Accelerated Innovation. (2020, June 10). *Business Wire.*

[7]Orland, K. (2020). TD Sees Big Role for AI in Fraud Detection, Lending Decisions. *Bloomberg.Com,* N.PAG. Retrieved from https://www.bloomberg.com/news/articles/2020-12-10/td-sees-big-role-for-ai-in-fraud-detection-lending-decisions

[8]How artificial intelligence in eCommerce can be a harbinger of next-gen customer experience? (2020, October 10). *Dataquest*, NA.

[9]Van Loo, R. (2019). Digital Market Perfection. *Michigan Law Review, 117*(5), 815–883.

[10]Graybeal, D. (2020). How to increase sales with artificial intelligence. *Marketing Artificial Intelligence Institute.* Retrieved from https://www.marketingaiinstitute.com/blog/how-to-increase-sales-with-artificial-intelligence

[11]Iansiti, M., & Lakhani, K. R. (2020). Competing in the Age of AI: Strategy and Leadership when Algorithms and Networks Run the World. *Harvard Business Review Press.*

[12]Lamontagne, N. D. (2020). AI Makes Processing Smarter: Advanced analytics of artificial intelligence lower costs and predict problems before they happen. *Plastics Engineering, 76*(9).

[13]Kovalenko, O. (2020). How to use AI and machine learning in fraud detection. Retrieved from https://spd.group/machine-learning/fraud-detection-with-machine-learning/

[14]United States: Aon to leverage Artificial Intelligence to help reduce workers compensation litigation costs. (2019, July 27). *TendersInfo News.*

[15]Baryannis, G., Validi, S., Dani, S., & Antoniou, G. (2019). Supply chain risk management and artificial intelligence: state of the art and future research

directions. *International Journal of Production Research, 57*(7), 2179–2202.

[16]Ricard, S. (2020). AI's effect on productivity now and in the future. *Forbes*. Retrieved from https://www.forbes.com/sites/forbestechcouncil/2020/03/20/ais-effect-on-productivity-now-and-in-the-future/?sh=3e7091997591

[17]How AI is increasing employee productivity. (2020). Retrieved from https://memory.ai/timely-blog/ai-increase-employee-productivity

[18]Morrison, C. (2019). Putting a voice to digital banking. *Independent Banker, 69*(3), 38–41. New White Paper Release and Top Medical Professionals Reveal How Artificial Intelligence (AI) Improves Patient Care and Reduces Costs. (2018, February 19). *M2 Presswire.*

[19]Blue-Collar AI Can Solve Skills Gap. (2019, May 15). *EHS Today (Online Exclusive).*

[20]Smith. C. (2019). An employee's best friend? How AI can boost employee engagement and performance. *Strategic HR Review, 18*(1), 17–20.

[21]Gautman, A. (2019). Artificial intelligence and employee engagement: Connecting the dots. The SHRM South Asia Blog. Retrieved from https://blog.shrm.org/sasia/blog/artificial-intelligence-and-employee-engagement-connecting-the-dots

[22]Huang, M.-H., & Rust, R. T. (2021). A strategic framework for artificial intelligence in marketing. *Journal of the Academy of Marketing Science, 49*(1), 30–50.

[23]Gehlber, A. (2020). 4 ways AI is changing Go To Market strategy. *AIThority*. Retrieved from https://aithority.com/challenges/4-ways-ai-is-changing-go-to-market-strategy/

[24]Davenport, T., Guha, A., Grewal, D., & Bressgott, T. (2020). How artificial intelligence will change the future of marketing. *Journal of the Academy of Marketing Science, 48*(1), 24–42.

[25]Gabelaia, I. (2020). Enhancing the Customer User Experience Through a Feedback-driven Conversational Marketing: Encouraging Superior Engagement. *Proceedings of the Multidisciplinary Academic Conference,* 36–49.

[26]Kaulins, K. (2020). How multilingual chatbots influence localization. *MultiLingual, 31*(3), 52–55.

[27]Slijepčević, M., Radojević, I., & Perić, N. (2020). Considering Modern Trends in Digital Marketing. *Marketing (0354-3471), 51*(1), 34–42.

[28]Sidaoui, K., Jaakkola, M. & Burton, J. (2020). (2020). AI feel you: customer experience assessment via chatbot interviews. *Journal of Service Management, 31*(4), 745–766.

[29]Benabdelouahed, M. R. & Dakouan, C. (2020). The Use of Artificial Intelligence in Social Media: Opportunities and Perspectives. *Expert Journal of Marketing, 8*(1), 82–87.

[30]Grover, V. (2020). What is the future of video marketing? Retrieved from https://www.martechadvisor.com/articles/interactive-marketing/what-is-the-future-of-video-marketing-2020-and-beyond/

[31]Doherty, D., & Curran, K. (2019). Chatbots for online banking services. *Web Intelligence (2405-6456), 17*(4), 327–342.

[32]Mhlanga, D. (2020). Industry 4.0 in Finance: The Impact of Artificial Intelligence (AI) on Digital Financial Inclusion. *International Journal of Financial Studies*, 3.

[33]Fourie, L., & Bennett, T. K. (2019). Super intelligent financial services. *Journal of Payments Strategy & Systems, 13*(2), 151–164.

[34]RHB Introduces Malaysia's First SME Financing Mobile App Powered By Artificial Intelligence. (2020, August 3). *Contify Banking News.*

[35]Tokic, D. (2018). BlackRock Robo-Advisor 4.0: When artificial intelligence replaces human discretion. *Strategic Change, 27*(4), 285–290.

[36]Raj, A. (2021). Artificial intelligence (AI) in supply chain and logistics supply. Retrieved from https://throughput.world/blog/ai-in-supply-chain-and-logistics/

[37]Larrabee, H. (2019, July 1). Retail Gets Smarter: These are the top ways artificial intelligence is changing the customer experience in retail. *Retail Merchandiser, 59*(4), 12.

[38]Polachowska, K. (2019). 10 use cases of AI in Manufacturing. Retrieved from https://neoteric.eu/blog/10-use-cases-of-ai-in-manufacturing/#:~:text= Accenture%20and%20Frontier%20Economics%20estimate,across%2016% 20industries%2C%20including%20manufacturing.&text=Let's%20have%20a% 20look%20at,of%20artificial%20intelligence%20for%20manufacturers.

[39]Wilmot, J. (2020). Artificial intelligence at the edge improves manufacturing productivity: AI at the plant floor's edge empowers machine builders to increase production quality and efficiency. *Plant Engineering, 74*(10), 44–48.

[40]Kaul, S. (2021). How artificial intelligence can accelerate and elevate digital transformation. *Skan.* Retrieved from https://www.skan.ai/process-mining-insights/how-artificial-intelligence-can-accelerate-and-elevate-digital-transformation

[41]Baltazar, A. (2019). Demystifying Artificial Intelligence: The question of AI isn't what it's going to do for grocery stores in the future--it's what it's not going to do. *Winsight Grocery Business, 85*(1), 99.

[42]Weber, F. D. & Schütte, R. (2019). State-of-the-art and adoption of artificial intelligence in retailing. Digital Policy, *Regulation and Governance, 21*(3), 264–279.

[43]Rueter, T. (2021). How AI Can Help With Assortment Planning: As food and consumables retailers grow more digital, they'll make use of ever more granular data to better forecast consumer demand. *Progressive Grocer, 100*(1), 76–80.

Chapter 4

[1]Day, J. (2016). How to convince your boss to invest in new technology. Retrieved from https://blog.trumpetinc.com/how-to-convince-your-boss-to-invest-in-new-technology

[2]Reim, W., Astrom, J. & Erikssom, O. (2020). Implementation of artificial

intelligence (AI): A roadmap for business model innovation. *AI 2020, 1*, 180–191;

[3]Langenkamp, J. (2020, December 22). The Importance of Data Strategy: Organizations need a clear road map for delivery of data architecture components that identifies priority-driven milestones and analytics capabilities. *Big Data Quarterly, 6*(4), 19.

[4]Marr, B. (2019a). How to create a data strategy: 7 things every business must include. Forbes. Retrieved from https://www.forbes.com/sites/bernardmarr/2019/03/11/how-to-create-a-data-strategy-7-things-every-business-must-include/?sh=226d8377218b

[5]Jinman, H. (2019). How to scale AI projects correctly. *Medium.* Retrieved from https://medium.com/@henry_66577/how-to-scale-ai-projects-correctly-1b9cf846e5d3

[6]Arlotto, P. (2020, February 1). Artificial intelligence: 5 realities for financial leaders: The first step in a healthcare organization's artificial intelligence strategy should be education. *Healthcare Financial Management, 74*(2), 32.

[7]Clayton, S. J. (2021). An Agile Approach to Change Management. *Harvard Business Review Digital Articles*, 2–5.

[8]Diorio. S. (2020). Realizing the growth potential of AI. *Forbes.* Retrieved from https://www.forbes.com/sites/forbesinsights/2020/05/08/realizing-the-growth-potential-of-ai/?sh=343540e633f3

[9]AI Has Complete Power Over the Customer Experience: Artificial intelligence and the data fed into it will be the key to good customer service. (2020, September 1). *CRM Magazine*, 24(7), 17.

[10]Marr, B. (2020a). How to develop an artificial intelligence strategy: 9 things every business must include. Bernard Marr. Retrieved from https://bernardmarr.com/default.asp?contentID=1858

[11]Marr, B. (2020b). How to develop you artificial intelligence (AI) strategy. Retrieved from https://bernardmarr.com/default.asp?contentID=1843

[12]Yao, M., Jia, M. & Zhou, A. (2018). *Applied Artificial Intelligence: A Handbook for Business Leaders*. TOPBOTS Inc.

[13]Iansiti, M., & Lakhani, K. R. (2020). *Competing in the Age of AI: Strategy and Leadership when Algorithms and Networks Run the World.* Harvard Business Review Press.

[14]Bias, racism and lies: facing up to the unwanted consequences of AI. *UN News.* Retrieved from https://news.un.org/en/story/2020/12/1080192

[15]Milkovich, D. (2020). 15 alarming cyber security facts and stats. Retrieved from https://www.cybintsolutions.com/cyber-security-facts-stats/

[16]Perlroth, N. (2017, October 3). All 3 Billion Yahoo Accounts Were Affected by 2013 Attack. *International New York Times.*

[17]Denning, P. J., & Denning, D. E. (2020). Dilemmas of Artificial Intelligence. *Communications of the ACM*, 63(3), 22–24.

[18]Duckett, C. (2021). Apple CEO sounds warning of algorithms pushing society towards catastrophe. *Zdnet.* Retrieved from https://www.zdnet.com/article/apple-ceo-sounds-warning-of-algorithms-

pushing-society-towards-catastrophe/?ftag=TRE6a12a91&bhid=294033385
206112571147340761739277&mid=13250610&cid=2272076622

[19]Marr, B. (2019b). The amazing ways YouTube uses artificial intelligence and machine learning. Forbes. Retrieved from https://www.forbes.com/sites/bernardmarr/2019/08/23/the-amazing-ways-youtube-uses-artificial-intelligence-and-machine-learning/?sh=29d6b0945852

[20]Matthews, J. (2020, March 22). Patterns and Antipatterns, Principles, and Pitfalls: Accountability and Transparency in Artificial Intelligence. *AI Magazine, 41*(1), 82.

Chapter 5

[1]Diorio. S. (2020). Realizing the growth potential of AI. *Forbes*. Retrieved from https://www.forbes.com/sites/forbesinsights/2020/05/08/realizing-the-growth-potential-of-ai/?sh=343540e633f3

[2]BasuMallick, C. (2019). 3 effective leadership skills you need in the age of AI. *HR Technologist*. Retrieved from https://www.hrtechnologist.com/author/chiradeep-basumallick/

[3]Shulstad, R. A., & Mael, R. D. (2010). Leading and managing through influence: Challenges and responses (senior leader perspective). *Air and Space Power Journal,* 24(2), 6-17.

[4]El Namaki, M. S. S. (2020). From Product to Function: The Strategic Artificial Intelligence Shift. *Scholedge International Journal of Business Policy & Governance, 7*(2), 19–24.

[5]Hobbib, W. (2019). Why business leaders can't afford to miss out on investing in artificial intelligence. Inc. Retrieved from https://www.inc.com/bill-hobbib/why-business-leaders-cant-afford-to-miss-out-on-investing-in-artificial-intelligence.html

Common AI terms

[1]Glossary of artificial intelligence. (2021). Retrieved from https://en.wikipedia.org/wiki/Glossary_of_artificial_intelligence#B

[2]Rouhiainen, L. Artificial Intelligence: 101 Things You Must Know Today About Our Future (Kindle). 2018. Retrieved from www.amazon.com

[3]Patrick, B., & Williams, K. L. (2020). What is artificial intelligence? *Journal of Accountancy, 229*(2), 1–4.

[4]Haenlein, M. & Kaplan, A. (2019). A Brief History of Artificial Intelligence: On the Past, Present, and Future of Artificial Intelligence. *California Management Review. 61*(4):5-14.

[5]Garwood, M. (2018). Ready or Not, Here Comes AI. *Broadcasting & Cable, 148*(17), 14–N.PAG.

[6]Pattern recognition. (2018). Encyclopaedia Britannica. Retrieved from https://www.britannica.com/technology/pattern-recognition-computer-science

ABOUT THE AUTHOR

Dr. Militza Basualdo is an international keynote speaker, management consultant, author, and Professor of Technology and Innovation at Tecnologico de Monterrey. As VP Executive Partner at Gartner Inc., Dr. Basualdo advised CIOs and CxOs of major corporations in eight countries. Dr. Basualdo held the CIO position for Procter & Gamble and Citibank in Mexico and Process Improvement director for Dell in the Americas and Metlife.

Dr. Basualdo holds a Doctorate in Management from the University of Phoenix, a Master of Science in Computer Science, and a Bachelor of Arts in Mathematics, Summa Cum Laude, both from Texas A&M University in Kingsville, Texas. Dr. Basualdo also holds a Lean Six Sigma Master Black Belt.

Are you interested in having your colleagues learn more about competing with AI? If you want to buy 10 or more copies, send me an email for available discounts at mbasualdo@accelencia.com.

Printed in Poland
by Amazon Fulfillment
Poland Sp. z o.o., Wrocław

78422866R00094